hand in Hand

A true-life story

Holly Otten

ISBN 978-0-615-45759-8

Text, Poems and Cover Design
By Holly Otten, unless otherwise noted.

Copyright ©2012

All rights reserved.

Printed in the United States.

All Biblical references are taken from the New International Version®, NIV®. Unless otherwise noted.

Scripture quotations marked (NIV) are taken from the Holy Bible, Copyright © 1973, 1978, 1984, 2011 by Biblica, Inc.™ Used by permission of Zondervan. All rights reserved worldwide. www.zondervan.comThe "NIV" and "New International Version" are trademarks registered in the United States Patent and Trademark Office by Biblica, Inc.™

Cover: Photography by Maria Cassaday

Note: Many of the person's names mentioned in this book have been changed out of respect for privacy.

Tools for Spirit-Led Living

Dedication

To my earthly angels…

My Auntie—Pauline
7·9·1924—4·11·2015
&
My Nana—Sophia
5·13·1912—10·30·2010

Much thanks to...

My Father, Jesus, my Savior, Holy Spirit—You are My Lord, my God, and my All.

Steve, my devoted husband—for his unfailing support and patience, and for the awesome ways that he loves me.

My three little men whom I adore—my life would be empty without you.

Bonnie Kennedy—my best friend in the whole-wide world.

Fr. John Randall—in loving memory—for sheltering me under his wing, for teaching me and molding me, for giving me a strong foundation in my faith, and for being an example of Christ. 12·31·1928−6·14·2011

Foreword

I have just concluded my testimony on how I overcame sexual abuse and neglect when I open things up to a Q & A session. The first question comes from a dark-haired woman sitting in the last row.

She seems a bit shy, but summons the courage to share her thoughts. "I love how God took the ashes of your life and turned it into something beautiful, as is promised in God's Word. This has been my prayer also."

A while later a robust, middle-aged man with soft eyes asks me, "How did you come to surrender yourself completely to God, the Father, who bears the likeness of your father, a man who abused you?"

The next question posed comes from a woman who reminds me of my grandmother. This petite, warm-eyed, gray-haired lady surprises me with her question, "I wonder how it is that you came to feel safe and at peace while being married to a man?"

As the Q & A session is drawing to a close, a woman holding a baby on her lap raises her hand to ask me, "How did you go from being a broken and unloved little girl to being a loving and nurturing mother to your three children?"

The answer to all of these questions is—GOD'S LOVE. ("God is love". 1 John 4:16).

Twenty years ago before I knew Christ, I received a small card from a Christian aunt that read, "The greatest joy in the world is to love and be loved." Those words when I first read them just rung in my heart. I kept this card on my bedroom mirror so that I was reminded of those words. I wanted those words to be fulfilled in my life. I was so deprived of love. I was thirsty for it, just like the Samaritan woman at the well in John 4, who sought love from many men, but was always left thirsty for more. I also knew that I did not have the ability to love.

After seeking love and fulfillment in all the wrong places, I decided to give God a try. As soon as I opened the door to my heart, God's love came flooding in. Once I knew God, I questioned Him, "You tell me to love my neighbor as myself. Well, I don't love myself, so how am I supposed to love others?" I wanted to obey God in this, but felt unable. So this was my steady prayer, *"Give me love, O God, that I can love another human being with all of my heart."* And He did. God filled me with so much of His love, that it healed the broken pieces of my heart, and flowed over into others.

Introduction

A scripture comes to my mind when I think about how in the very beginning of my life, the devil tried to separate me from the love of God. Romans 8:35-39 explains the way that I see things:

> "Who shall separate us from the love of Christ? Shall trouble or hardship or persecution or famine or nakedness or danger or sword?...No, in all these things we are more than conquerors through him who loved us. For I am convinced that neither death nor life, neither angels nor demons, neither the present nor the future, nor any powers, neither height nor depth, nor anything else in all creation, will be able to separate us from the love of God that is in Christ Jesus our Lord."

This is the truth that I am so grateful my God has opened my eyes to see. God loved me at that very first moment when He created me, and He had a plan for me, one that didn't include being abused or neglected. Jeremiah 29:11 states, "For I know the plans I have for you,' declares the LORD, 'plans to prosper you and not to harm you, plans to give you hope and a future."

Sexual abuse and the pain it causes is not a happy topic to deal with. But, it is time to take what was bad and turn it into something good. I found this truth in Romans 8:28 "And we know that in all things God works for the good of those who love him."

At this time in my life, God is equipping and enabling me to bring comfort, encouragement and healing to others. God is using the pain of my past to bring comfort to others in the present. This brings me to think on Paul's words in 2 Corinthians 1:3 "…the Father of compassion and the God of all comfort, comforts us in all our troubles; so that we can comfort those in any trouble with the comfort we ourselves receive from God."

My desire is that my story, which tells of overcoming the affects of abuse and neglect, as well as many other obstacles, may fill you with the comfort that I have received; and with hope—based on the knowledge that what God has done for me, He will do for you—if you will just let Him.

The Tear Collector

My Father is in the business of collecting tears
He has a jar for every one of His children
When He sees His child's teardrop fall
He runs swiftly to catch it in a jar
Thus He is never far from them
Each tear is precious to Him
It sprang from the heart of His precious child

My Father is in the business of sharing
He shares the heavy loads His children bear
He said, "Come to Me all you who are weary
And I will give you rest"[1]
So when you feel you can't go on
Just ask the Father
He will share it with you

Now that I've come to know Him
I know this to be true
I was never alone in the midst of my suffering
When my father abused me, He was there
When my mother neglected me, He was there too
He collected every one of my tears
As a child collects treasures in a tiny tin box

My Father is in the business of compassion
Compassion- a feeling of sadness because
Of another's trouble or suffering
God sent His only Son to die a horrible death
Death on a cross for me and you

God the Father reached down from His throne
To come along side us out of compassion
He sent Jesus as a representative of Him
To know Jesus is to know the Father
To know Jesus is to know compassion and love
When Jesus met the widow who lost her son
He was moved with pity for her and said
Do not weep

God's Word tells us
He had to become like his brothers
In every way so that He might be merciful
He himself offered loud cries and tears to the
Father who was able to save him from death

As Jesus was lifted up so might we be
As we trust in Him with our burdens
Pains, disappointments, and sorrows
Let us embrace God the Father
The Tear Collector

"Put my tears in Your bottle. Are they not in Your book?"
Psalm 56:8. NAS

Beauty

*"To bestow on them a crown of **beauty**
for ashes" Isaiah 61:3*

Prologue

*As I lay in bed, my clock reads 12:00 a.m. I am only now realizing that a miracle happened tonight! God healed me! God had done what I had believed He would do—what I had prayed in earnest these last twenty-two months. I realize that when I was praising God while singing in the service tonight, I had stretched my arms heavenward for...at least forty minutes! Yet I felt **no pain**! And I must have stood for at least an hour, yet I felt **no fatigue**!*

God healed me of fibromyalgia and chronic fatigue!

Illness fell on me in October 2007. But as before, my Heavenly Father spoke to me ahead of time and told me that I was going to suffer. He did this at a time when I had gathered with a friend to pray. Things were so good at the time because Steve and I had gotten married only six months before. The kids seemed settled and our home was one of peace, joy and love. Life was everything that I had desired it to be. I actually thought that the message of suffering was for my friend and not for me.

Within a few weeks, I was given a book called, *90 Minutes in Heaven* by Don Piper, in which the autobiographer suffered immensely with pain due to a devastating car crash. Come to find out, God used this book to prepare me for the suffering that I was to endure. Shortly after I finished Piper's book, I began to experience severe pain throughout my entire body.

At the onset of this illness, while at a church service, I remember standing there trying to listen to the sermon. I was unable however, because the pain that I felt in my joints was unbearable. When it came time to turn around to shake hands with my neighbor behind me, the pain of that action brought tears to my eyes. The woman whose eyes I met placed her hand on my shoulder and tried to comfort me, but unbeknownst to her, she caused me more pain.

No one was able to touch me without causing me to flinch. Lying down in bed at night caused me pain because of the contact my body made with the mattress. The pain I felt dwelt in the muscles surrounding my joints, but particularly in the area of the back of my neck and shoulders. There were many days that I had to hold my head up with my hands because of the pain and energy it took to keep it up. It also caused me severe pain to lift my arms. It became very difficult to open the kitchen cupboards to prepare a meal for my family, put on a shirt, or lift my arms to shave in the shower. I couldn't lift my two year old Richard anymore or carry him in my arms.

Another symptom that surfaced was fatigue, and then depression followed. One seemed to magnify the other, so it became a vicious cycle. I was tired because I couldn't sleep at night from pain. The fatigue and pain caused depression. Depression was something I had been dealing with over the years and I had to struggle with it especially at this time. Because of the severe fatigue I felt, I was unable to stand for more than fifteen minutes at a time. On a good day, I lasted until 3:00 p.m. when I needed to drop onto the sofa or into my bed for the rest of the day. On a bad day, I didn't get out of bed at all.

    I went through countless tests by various doctors for an entire year. They ruled out everything, leaving them to conclude I had fibromyalgia and chronic fatigue. These two disorders frequently accompany the other and are not detectable in concrete tests. The doctors prescribed many "cocktails" to me over the course of my illness. I was given a medication to sleep in the evening, and then another one in the morning to stay awake. I had to take pain medication in the a.m. and p.m. I also had to increase the anti-depressants that I was on. For the last year, I took six medications around the clock that seemed to keep things at bay, but did not eliminate the symptoms completely. I also tried all sorts of natural remedies and none made much of an impact.

    I knew God was with me through my trial of illness, and therefore I trusted in Him. When the pain was severe, I'd think of the man I read about. He had it much worse than me. Then I became friends with a middle-aged woman who was battling cancer. She had similar symptoms as mine, but it had to be worse for her because she was fighting for her life. Knowing there were others who suffered more than me caused me to be grateful. I thanked God for the blessings in my life. This helped me to endure. God also gave me little miracles that assured me of His love and His presence in my life. There are two of them that stand out in my mind the most.

The first one happened on Easter morning. Prior to that morning, I had been experiencing a very difficult time, which ironically was the Church season of Lent. The darkness and constant chill of the winter added to my pain and weary soul. Many times I found myself turning to God and begging for His help. I was reminded of the scripture, "The Lord is my light and my salvation" (Psalm 27:1), and prayed that He would shine His light into my darkness. He answered my prayer on Easter morning.

During Lent I had passed a church that displayed a sign by the road that read, "Sunrise Service on Easter morning." I had always wanted to attend a sunrise service on Easter. I had never been to this church before, but on Easter morning I woke Steve and my three young children at 6:00 a.m. in order to attend the sunrise service. The temperature was in the high thirties so I bundled up my children and brought blankets to wrap them. It was a beautiful, joy-filled service which included the Living Passion.

As we were leaving the service, I noticed the sun rising above the tree line. I thought it appropriate to take a picture of the sunrise so I took two pictures. Later that day I downloaded the pictures onto my computer. As my husband and I viewed the pictures of the sun blown up on the screen, we noticed something curious about the second picture that I took. There was a white image in the sky. My husband said to me, "It looks like the Risen Christ." In that same picture there were sunbeams that formed a cross, and a red diamond appeared on the cross. None of these things appeared in the first picture which I took less than a minute earlier.

    I prayed and asked God if this was a sign of His presence and He brought me to a scripture in the Bible entitled, "The Transfiguration." He showed me the verse that states, "His (Jesus) face shone like the sun, and His clothes became white as light" (Matthew 17:2). Immediately, I knew that God had given me a gift. I had been praying for His light, and He came in the form of light, during the rising of the Easter sun.

    The second miracle happened several months later while Steve and I were celebrating our anniversary, by vacationing at an inn on the harbor. While there, I had taken pictures of every sunrise and sunset. It seemed that I had taken pictures of everything and everyone on this trip, except on one particular evening. Steve and I decided to walk the beach under the light of the moon. It was the only time that I didn't have my camera because I had left it back at the inn. The moon was making a grand show of itself and I so desired to have a picture of it. I was really kicking myself for forgetting it.

The next morning I rose to take pictures of the sunrise which we could see from the window of our room. After the sun had fully risen, and it shown amidst a bright blue sky, I got up to put my camera away. However, from a different view I spotted the moon which still shown faintly in the sky. I decided to take a picture of it. When my digital camera revealed the picture in its small screen, it depicted a bright moon in a black sky! It was hard to believe what my eyes were showing me because the moon that I took a picture of floated amidst a bright blue, sunny sky. I showed my husband, and then the caretaker of the inn, both of whom possess knowledge of photography. Neither one could explain the picture scientifically. I knew then that my Father in Heaven, who is present on this earth, gave me a gift. God gave me the picture of the moon that I so wanted the night before.

After six months of severe pain and fatigue, I felt God calling me to pray for healing. I began asking others to pray over me by the laying on of hands. I believe in the power of the laying on of hands just as the early Christians did, as well as Jesus Himself. In Mark 6:5,6 it says, "So He (Jesus) was not able to perform any mighty deeds there, apart from curing a few sick people by *laying His hands on them."*

I began looking for scripture verses that spoke of healing. One verse that I claimed as my own is from Mark 5:25-34 about the woman afflicted with hemorrhaging. In verse 34 Jesus states, "Your faith has healed you." Again and again I read throughout the New Testament these words. Therefore I was reminded that I could only be healed if I truly believed that Jesus could heal me. I started to thank God and praise Him for healing me.

Seventeen years had passed since God gave me the scripture about the "wings of an eagle" and brought me out of the pit of emotional illness. Once again, while suffering from physical illness, I found myself clinging to that very scripture promise found in Isaiah 40:29-31,

> "He gives strength to the fainting; for the weak He makes vigor abound. Though young men faint and grow weary, and youths stagger and fall, they that hope in the Lord will renew their strength, they will soar as with eagles' wings; they will run and not grow weary, walk and not grow faint."

I kept this verse above my kitchen sink and would read it, pray it, and believe it. I would cling to it in the midst of trying to summon the strength to cook a meal or as I rolled out of bed with my three year old tugging at me, "Mommy, get up. The sun is out. It's time to get up."

I always felt that God was using my time of suffering for good reasons. I've come to believe that one of the fruits that came from this period was my first book which I wrote and published.

In July 2009, after fifteen months of praying for healing, God revealed something to me. He gave me the words from 2 Kings 20:1-5 entitled "Hezekiah's Illness." Hezekiah was told by God that he was about to die from his illness. In response, Hezekiah prayed to the Lord, "O Lord, remember how faithfully and wholeheartedly I conducted my life in your presence, doing what is pleasing to you!" And then he wept bitterly. God then told Isaiah to tell Hezekiah, "I have heard your prayer and seen your tears. I will heal you." I felt that God told me then that He was going to heal me. I even wrote it expectantly in my journal.

One week later I sat down with my boys to pray together. As usual, I asked one of them to open the Bible and choose something to read aloud. Using his personal Bible, my twelve year old Gabriel read the exact same scripture from 2 Kings 20. I shared with the boys that God had spoken that verse to me a week earlier and I believed that He was going to heal me of my illness. We then praised God ahead of time, "Thank you for healing Mama!"

A week later, while attending a Christian conference in Florida, God gave me the same verse for a third time. While sitting and listening to a speaker, the verse that God gave me came to my mind. I decided to open up to it to read again but couldn't remember which chapter in Kings it was in. Surprisingly, I opened right up to the exact page of 2 Kings 20. The following evening I found myself doing things that I hadn't been able to do in twenty-two months!

God gave me confirmation of my healing a few days later while still at the conference. While in prayer with a woman who didn't know anything about me, my illness, healing, or the scripture that I clung to, something amazing happened. As we prayed with our eyes closed, I heard her speak the promise that I had been clinging to from Isaiah 40, about "eagles' wings." I then had a vision. I saw an eagle flying—it was the biggest eagle I'd ever seen. Its wing span was about twenty feet. I knew that it was me soaring with the wings of an eagle. Concluding our prayer, I told her that the scripture she mentioned spoke to me personally. She said in reply, "I had a vision of the largest eagle I have ever seen soaring in the sky." We had experienced the same vision at the same time.

At the end of the conference, I felt as if I could make it back home from Florida to Rhode Island without the aid of a mechanical machine with wings. On returning, I weaned myself off the medication and continually regained my strength. I began celebrating lots of "firsts" since becoming ill. For almost two years I couldn't do any of the things that I loved to do, including play with my boys. I celebrated the *first* time playing Frisbee with my boys, the *first* time playing tennis with oldest son, the *first* time dancing with my best friend, and the *first* time hiking with my husband.

I reveled in the simple things, such as tinkering in my flower garden and cooking for my family. The first Saturday upon my return from Florida, I spent five hours baking and cooking. What a relief for Steve and the kids to not have to eat frozen foods seven days a week. On Sunday, I spent the day boating with my family, where I was able to swim, and even go tubing. Alleluia! My God is a God of miracles! This coming August will mark the third year of being free from illness.

God is good! He is faithful! But, I am reminded of what He told me while in Florida following my healing. I very clearly felt Him say to me, "Your faith has healed you." This brought to mind the other scripture promise from Mark 5:34 that I had also been claiming. Jesus told the woman with the issue of blood, "Daughter, your faith has healed you. Go in peace and be freed from your suffering." God brought to fruition this promise that I had clung to, just as 2 Thessalonians 1:11 states, "We pray that God powerfully bring to fruition every effort of faith."

I have learned through my illness and healing the need to believe and have faith in what I pray for. I also learned the importance of asking. I suffered illness for at least six months without asking God to heal me. It wasn't until God urged me to pray for healing that I did so. Until that moment, I accepted it as if I deserved to be ill.

Over and over again in the New Testament, people in need would come to Jesus. He made it a point to ask them, "What do you want?" This is an interesting question because Jesus is God and He knows everything. He required that they ask. In Matthew 20:32, Jesus asked two blind men, "What do you want me to do for you?" In response to them, because Jesus is God and God is love, He healed them. In verse 34 it says, "Moved with pity, Jesus touched their eyes." I am so glad that my God is a God of compassion and mercy. He healed me when I asked Him and I am truly grateful.

Ashes

*"To bestow on them a crown of beauty for **ashes**" Isaiah 61:3*

Chapter One

I cannot wiggle my toes or kick my tiny feet. I can't move from my waist down. I can't even curl up in my favorite fetal position. I wish my mommy would cuddle with me and hold me tight. Am I a thing? Maybe I'm a doll. Dolls don't have feelings. But I do! Someone hold me!

I was born in Providence, RI in 1966 with a dislocated hip. I was delicate and awkward to hold for months because of the body cast that went from my feet to my chest. Even though I wasn't soft and cuddly to hold, you would think my mother would have still desired to hold me. I don't remember much at this young age, but what I do know is that my mother's affections that I so longed for were missing. Even when the cast was removed from my small body, my mother still didn't hold me.

I learned later on in life that Mom herself wasn't nurtured by her parents. Her father was an alcoholic and her mother was busy chasing the affections of men.

When I was born, I joined my brother Michael who was three years old at the time. My parents didn't have much money. My father hadn't a higher education; he was a self-taught car mechanic. My mother was a licensed nurse. I heard that things weren't so good back then. Dad's extra-curricular activities involving women and the drink drove Mom to leave him by the time my sister Elizabeth arrived on the scene. I was two years old. Mom had no patience left for my father's abusive ways and his adventures that included taking off for weeks at a time with female friends. My mother brought my sister into the world without my father at her side. When she arrived home with their new baby girl, she found him in bed with another woman.

Since my father did not provide for his children, Mom tried to get public assistance to provide for her family. She was turned down because they felt she was over qualified. However, her job did not provide for her family of four. She felt overwhelmed with her circumstances and made an agreement with her best friend who was single and childless that she would take care of Elizabeth until Mom's circumstances got better.

Mom got Elizabeth back when she was two years old. It wasn't easy though. Mom's friend ran away with Elizabeth because she didn't want to part with her. None of us children knew this story until Elizabeth accidentally found out when she was in her late thirties. What is ironic is that Elizabeth always felt that she was adopted. She always doubted that my mother and father were her biological parents. She never felt like she belonged or was loved by them.

Even though we didn't have much growing up, and Mom worked way too much, I am grateful that she didn't stay with my father. Things would have definitely been worse for our family. My father was an angry, explosive, violent, and abusive man. Later on in life, God revealed to me that I stored hatred and fear of men inside of me, and that it began while I was still in the womb. It makes sense to me because my father was abusive towards my mother, and as the child being carried in her womb, sharing the same life source and environment, it's no wonder I felt what my mother felt.

My father was verbally, physically, and sexually abusive. When my mother left my father she no longer was the victim of his abuse. Unfortunately though, my father had visitation rights with us which entailed weekends, school vacations, and summers. My siblings and I hated to go with my father and step-mother. My father remarried almost immediately after he divorced. He married a fifteen year old girl, ten years his junior, the one with whom he was cheating with last, while married to my mother.

During those visits, my dad did crazy, unhealthy things like make us sit at the table for hours to eat foods that we didn't like. One time my brother vomited in his tomato soup, but my father made him eat it anyway. Dad was always critical; always demanding, like a master to a slave; always negative; and always full of rage. Oh, he said "I love you" and hugged us—but we didn't feel his love, and he was altogether too touchy. My mother never said those three words that a child longs to hear, and she didn't hold us close or shower her affections on us. She did the opposite of my father. Mom neglected us. Dad molested us.

Part of the neglect was due to the fact that Mom worked two or three jobs to support us. She didn't spend money on herself or spend her nights partying on the town. She just wasn't there. She wasn't there to cook us meals, and if she was, we had TV dinners. Mom didn't cook or clean. My siblings and I were usually alone for dinner, so we might've grabbed a raw hotdog or chocolate-chip cookies to eat.

I remember those nights when it was late out, dark, and lonely; wondering when Mom would come home. It was scary being alone, even though we had each other. There was no adult to protect us. One evening at dusk my siblings and I were playing ball in the street, as we always did. As I ran out between two parked cars to chase after a ball, an adult biker was speeding by and rammed right into my forehead. My brother brought me into the house and tried to aid me and my injury. I remember wanting my mommy so badly. But she wasn't there. She was working. My mom felt more comfortable in the role of nurse than she did as mother.

My sister and I were often left under the supervision of our brother which wasn't always good. He behaved in many ways just as our father did.

Some nights Michael played a game with me. Later I learned he played it with my sister too. We played it in the dark, in my mother's room on her bed. It entailed oral sex. I know that I was under the age of ten because it didn't happen after we moved to Florida. I don't put too much blame on my brother because he was young. I put more of the blame on my father, because I believe my father abused my brother and that is where Michael learned such behavior.

As a child, I was very sickly. I was extremely thin and pale, so much so that people were always asking if I felt sick. Much of the time I could answer yes to that question. I was also physically weak, as I had anemia, resulting in low energy. I was emotionally frail and tended to faint when I became stressed. As an adult, I look back at these facts and feel that the sexual abuse and neglect I endured caused me to be this way. I was carrying a disease in my heart that no one could see, but it revealed itself every time I became ill. Every time a virus came around, I got it, and each instance would put me in bed for days. I was frequently in the hospital receiving tests and a ton of blood work. I often felt like a pin cushion.

Considering my personality, I am again led to think of weakness. I was deathly shy and always hiding behind my mother's leg when I was around a stranger. I behaved like a mouse, always afraid of everyone and everything. I guess you could say that I behaved like a wounded animal—afraid, hurting and bearing wounds, but unable to voice it.

During those early years living in Providence, there were two blessings which I credit my mom for—one is the Catholic school she sent us to, and the other, our day care provider whom we called "Auntie." My father's mother was a very devoted Catholic and pressured my mother to send us to a Catholic School. My mother was not a devoted Christian and never was. I think the grace of God had something to do with this circumstance.

My siblings and I loved that school. It was our family; our safe place. We felt loved and cared for when we were there, and we had lots of friends. This is where I became familiar and comfortable in God's house, which at the time was the Catholic Church. As a school we went to church across the street at least once a week. This is when the seed of faith was planted; where my faith began.

The other blessing was our caregiver Pauline, otherwise known as Auntie. I bet just about everyone has an "Auntie," an aunt or person who has been a special part of their life. I have an Auntie, but she's not a blood relative. Anyone twenty years younger who knows Auntie uses this endearing term. Pauline won my heart at the young age of six weeks, when my Mom took me to her. She became "My Auntie" right then, and I still call her Auntie today. I look back at all of the years I've known her, and realize that God sent her to me. She is like an earthly angel. In the midst of a dark and scary childhood, God had shown His love and care for me through her. He knew I needed her.

Auntie took care of me and my siblings from 8 a.m. to 5 p.m., five days a week. I wasn't easy to care for because of my body cast. Auntie took such good care of my cast by keeping it clean, and my skin healthy, that my doctor had commented on it to my mother. Auntie didn't just watch us kids. She was the parent we didn't have.

If you were a fly on the wall, forty years ago, when I was in the care of Auntie, you might have observed any one of these scenes: Auntie under the kitchen table playing with a few children…rocking one of us in her rocking chair…teaching us how to make home-made apple pies…helping us to make a craft as a Christmas present for our moms…holding our hands as she walked us to school…or teaching us how to sew.

One memory that I often razz Auntie with is how she forced us to go out into winter's frigid temperatures. Auntie would bundle us up so that we felt like statues and shoo us out the door. After five minutes we'd come knocking on the door and tell her, "We're cold and we're bored. Let us come in." Auntie would always respond with, "Go chase the wind!" We immediately ran to the corner where the house and a stockade fence met, and huddled on top of one another, so as to share the warmth of each other's bodies.

These scenes are heartwarming, but you might have also observed Auntie reprimanding "her" kids. At times she held up a big wooden paddle and tapped it on her hand as she threatened to use it on a naughty child. (As an adult I found out that Auntie hadn't used that paddle one time. She never had to.) Sometimes if her kids were using their mouths in a naughty way, she would make them eat something awful tasting. Once, and only once, Auntie spanked my bottom over her knee. Today, I look at that as a loving act. She did what my parents should've done, had they been present. Auntie gave me what I needed, emotionally and physically, and I knew she loved me in all situations.

All of the kids Auntie cared for loved her like family. Once, when my sister was around six years old, we were alone and being looked after by our brother. My sister became upset and ran to Auntie's house crying and seeking her comfort. Auntie had an "Open House." It was as if she had a revolving door. Just about every neighbor on our street visited Auntie at least every few days.

When one walked into Auntie's house they were warmly welcomed with a smile and a hug. Because Auntie is from England, the kettle would be heated for tea. A chair would be pulled up, and food would be served. It didn't matter what time a visitor came. There would always be hot tea and something homemade. If it wasn't meal time, then there would be cookies—and lots of them. Auntie had Tupperware containers full of homemade cookies such as: chocolate-chip, salty peanut, molasses, fig, sugar and maple sugar.

My mother, as well as other parents, loved how Auntie leant a listening ear, a shoulder to cry on, and her years of wisdom. Auntie had lots of wisdom to offer. She grew up in the midst of World War II in England. She left everyone and everything she knew when she became a "War Bride," and moved to the United States to live with her husband. They didn't have much and they had six children to support. At one time, Auntie cared for her husband's two ailing parents in her own home. She cared for them until they passed, all the while, caring for her own young children, as well as her day care children.

Auntie has always showed me that she knew and loved Jesus. As a child I saw her live like Jesus. Over the years, I've observed Auntie's faith in action. Her faith got her through many tough times. In times of hardship, I have seen how Auntie finds her strength in God. I have witnessed how she always finds something or someone to be grateful to God for, even in the midst of great sorrow or suffering. Understandably, I have accepted her God as mine too. It was her example of Christ's love that has stuck with me over all these years.

More seeds of faith sewn into my heart.

Auntie cared for me until I was ten years old. But I, as well as many other day care children, kept in touch and visited Auntie whenever we were in the vicinity. My siblings and I realized how much we appreciated Auntie once we moved. Thereafter, my mother felt my brother old enough to watch me and my sister, so that's all we had—each other. It really wasn't enough. Auntie, and all that she represented, was sorely missed.

Mom spoke for years about moving to sunny Florida. I think she had visions of the grass being greener there. She finally uprooted us and planted us in the area of Fort Lauderdale, Florida. "Sunny Florida" was hell for me. From the age of ten to the age of twelve and a half, when I left my family in Florida, life seemed unbearable. My mother had to work even more because of the cost of the move.

I remember at least two different occasions when we didn't see Mom for days. She worked a day job at the hospital, and then evening jobs doing home care for elderly patients. We lived in a lower-class neighborhood populated by mostly single-parent families. My peers were like me—left to care for themselves, with no supervision or the attention which we so desperately needed from our parents.

I was in the midst of puberty with my hormones raging, in an environment of peers running recklessly.

I found it hard to make friends. The kids I met were tough and hard. I was introduced to my mother's friend's daughter, but she was not the kind of girl a "healthy" parent would want their child to hang out with. She broke every commandment in the Bible. I succumbed to peer-pressure from her and her friends and began smoking pot. After a while, I liked the way I felt when I was high. It made me forget my feelings; like I didn't have a care in the world.

 I remember a few times when various parents for whom I babysat, got me high on pot. I got to the point that I would try anything anyone gave me, including many kinds of narcotics, just so I could escape my world. One day stands out in my mind when I took a large amount of aspirin so that I would be sick and cause Mom to stay home and nurse me. It worked. I reveled in Mom's affections as she sat on the edge of my bed crooning over me and then wiping my sweaty brow after vomiting in the toilet bowl. It was the only time Mom showed us affection, when we were sick. Mom played her role of nurse best.

 During this two year period, I skipped school a lot. Twice I skipped school for two weeks in a row. When my mother received phone calls at work, she felt that she couldn't leave her job. When Mom did see me, she rarely said anything except to question me about it. That was it—just a question. I answered her with a lie, and she left it at that. Since there wasn't anyone home to love me or to set restrictions, I stayed out until the early hours of the morning, hanging out with friends, which included eighteen year old men.

When I was home, I wasn't very pleasant. I behaved around my family like an angry monster. I was so miserable. Deep inside I just wanted to be loved and cared for. I wanted someone to hold me; to say that they loved me. I would beat up my sister, scream at my mother (when she was home), and have fist fights with my brother. Michael would try to tell me what to do as a parent would and I would behave like a rebellious teenager, even though I was yet a teen. He would use physical force on me to try to enforce his will on me. He would punch, slap, or shove me, and I would return a punch for a punch. We had horrible fights. This also caused me much misery. I hated my brother at the time.

I began fantasizing about how I could leave home. I wanted an exit from the life I was living in. I envisioned running away. I tried to come up with a successful plan, but found none. Oh, but there *was* a way to escape my life as I knew it, and it had to do with my father. The idea came from my mother, although I don't think she meant what she said. Sometimes when my mother got angry at us she would say, "You should go live with your father!"

My father and step-mother Donna had told us kids that if we ever wanted to live with them we were welcome. They couldn't have kids of their own, so they had a house with three empty bedrooms. At the age of twelve, during Christmas vacation, I said goodbye to the only family I knew. I couldn't have left quicker, but I later found out that I broke the hearts of my mother, brother and sister.

Chapter Two

I've been searching... searching... searching. Like the orphan boy Oliver Twist, as he sang the words "Where is love?" I've searched for it in countless men...they only take advantage of me. This ardent longing to be loved and validated, but to no avail, has led me to drown my pain in alcohol, smoking pot, popping narcotics, and snorting cocaine.

    I lived with my father and step-mother Donna in Portsmouth, RI from the age of twelve until the age of nineteen. Dad, like Mom, didn't know how to love. The only person he treated with love and respect was his mother, my Nana. Dad treated people as if they were inferior to him; as if their opinions didn't matter. My father was intimidating. He liked to have the upper hand. Dad never talked with me, always at me. He never asked me how my day was. He never praised me for the good things I accomplished. He always commented on the things I didn't do, or could've done better.

    Dad didn't connect with others. He was just like my mother. Mom was an island. Dad was a fortress—on guard at all times, weapons in hand. And those fiery darts flew through the air on a regular basis. Sometimes there were explosions. Dad was a man filled with rage. Anger was a part of him. One couldn't give a description of my father without mention of anger.

Before I arrived to live with Dad, Donna was Dad's scapegoat. When I came into the picture, I became Dad's scapegoat. Just about at the end of every work day, Dad came through the door ready to release his tension and anger on his scapegoat—me. I might have been smaller, weaker, the daughter of his making. No matter—his wrath had to fall somewhere. It fell on me.

Every day before Dad came home I had to have the house clean. I had to help with dinner and clean up the kitchen following dinner. I had to wait on Dad until he went to bed for the evening. If Dad walked in the door, and I didn't peel the potatoes correctly, Dad's rage came at me—maybe even the cutting board and potato peeler as well. Dad didn't physically abuse me as he did Mom. I remember only a few times when he shoved me across the room. I spent many hours in my bedroom where I tried to stay clear of my father and his controlling, angry, and abusive ways.

I feared my father—I feared his rage. Even so, I still behaved like a rebellious teen towards him. There was always a fight in me—with my brother and my father. I couldn't let them get away with treating me badly, so I spoke up. It always got me into worse trouble, but I didn't care. It led to very long screaming matches between my father and me (much like my brother and me) which ended up with me losing privileges, what little I had.

My father lacked moral character. He liked to party. He liked to drink. He even gave me alcohol when we had a house party, such as during a festive occasion. He didn't just offer me wine or beer. He offered me what he was drinking—the hard stuff. He even smoked pot on occasion, I had learned.

My father used curse words around me and told vulgar jokes. He walked around with almost nothing on, and didn't think anything of it to walk naked from his bedroom to the bathroom. My father was very touchy with me, as well as other women or children. He had sexual mannerisms; always flirting, always hugging and kissing; sometimes in the wrong places. My father managed to cheat on Donna as well as my mom, but she was too dependent on him to leave. She chooses to live in denial, like the rest of my father's family.

I can think of some positive things that I can attribute to Dad. Dad liked to have fun. He was also adventurous. When my siblings and I were with Dad, he did fun things with us, such as camping, boating, fishing, and traveling. Dad was talented in many ways and was filled with self-confidence. He had the attitude that he could do anything and do it better than anyone else. He behaved like a man who feared nothing and no one. These traits I secretly admired. My mother was opposite of my father in this way and I knew I didn't want to be like my mother. I saw Mom as a mouse. Mice can get squished very easily.

My parents were opposite in so many ways. They were at extreme ends of the spectrum. In all aspects of life, Mom was a pushover, and Dad, a steamroller. Mom was too lenient; Dad was too strict. I am grateful that I got to live with both of my parents in each environment. As I grew into an adult, I was able to take from each of these extreme life experiences and acquire what I believe is a healthy balance.

Overall, I found the influences around me to be positive while living with Dad. The positive influences in my life overpowered the negative ones, most of which were derived from my father. I found life in Portsmouth to be a great improvement from life in Florida. I was now living in a middle-class suburban town where most of my friends had both parents living at home, attended church on Sundays, and shared a prayer at mealtime. The school system was also a great improvement. I was also receiving love and attention from Donna, my Nana, and other relatives.

Nana, my father's mother, was my biggest support and had the greatest influence on me while living with Dad. Nana's house was a place of refuge for me. I hated my father and sought ways to get away from him, usually by visiting family members. They were about the only people he would let me socialize with.

I spent many of my weekends soaking up Nana's love, affection, and good cooking! Nana was another person whom God shone His love through; another earthly angel. She was kind, gentle, and very giving. Every evening as dinner concluded, my grandparents would sit at the table and lead me in praying the rosary.

When I was troubled about something I could share it with Nana and she would pray with me. One time when I was talking to her on the phone, she had noticed that I sounded downcast. I told her, "When I was visiting my Mom in Florida I met a boy whom I like very much. I miss him so much Nana." Nana didn't tell me I was too young to be involved with boys. She told me, "Just talk to God and tell Him how you feel." After I hung up the phone, I did just what Nana suggested, and soon after, I noticed that I felt better. The pain in my heart wasn't as great.

Nana prayed from the moment her eyes opened until the moment they closed again at the end of her day. Nana, however, didn't just speak the words of a Christian. She continually showed me what it meant to live like Jesus.

Most of my relatives from both sides of the family lived in Rhode Island. This enabled me to reap the benefits that a child gets from the love and stability of having family relationships. This was an element that was missing when my mother moved us to Florida. Mom knew no one when she moved us there, and so we had no support from anyone.

My step-mother Donna and I got along very well. She didn't have kids, so I was the child she never had. She is ten years younger than my father so we could relate pretty well with one another. As I matured, we became more like friends. My father didn't let me do much socially, so Donna and I would hang out together. We'd go shopping, see a movie, or get a bite to eat. Outside of that, I was made to stay home most of the time. I hated it at the time that my father always had to have me within his grasp, but it was actually a good thing for me. It kept me from getting into trouble.

By the time I was a junior in high school I was doing pretty well for myself. I was a good student in school, and enjoyed using my talents in Art classes and Chorus. I got a job working every day after school until 7:00 p.m. serving food at the Salve Regina College cafeteria. This enabled me to buy my own car. My self-esteem was gradually improving. I even started to have a social life. I told Dad that if he didn't start letting me go out with friends, including dating, that I would go live with my mother. He relented, but with a strict curfew. I had to be home by 11:00 p.m. and could only go out on the weekends. This enabled me to mingle in the social scenes and soon after, I became popular with a wide circle of girls and boys.

My junior year was special because it is when I met my best friend Bonnie. I met Bonnie while searching for accompaniment for the annual variety show. I wanted to sing in the show but wouldn't dare do it acapella! A mutual friend introduced us and we've been inseparable ever since. The night of the show, Bonnie played piano and I sang my heart out to Carole King's "So Far Away." It was an awesome experience for me!

I feel that over the years God put people in my life that would help direct me on the right path; to be models from whom I could I learn from. Bonnie is one of those people. I have always felt this to be important, especially due to the fact that I lacked good and loving models in my own parents.

Bonnie was raised in a completely opposite environment than me. Her parents, who showed love towards each other, raised her and her three sisters with morals and family values. I feel Bonnie is a gift from God, even though she and I have never shared our beliefs. Bonnie was raised as a Jehovah's Witness and by the time I began walking my faith, she left hers. Hence, she didn't influence me in this aspect. However, Bonnie has always behaved like a Christian, more so than many self-professed Christians who attend church regularly, like my father.

Dad attended church every Sunday, but his behaviors were all but holy. Dad, having been brought up in a strict Catholic family, dragged me to church every week. All through high school Dad woke me up every Sunday to get to the 8:00 a.m. service! We'd sit through the service until the closing hymn began, and then whoosh! Dad was running out the door, so to escape the parking lot traffic. We'd practically knock pedestrians over as we peeled wheels out onto the street.

Dad tried to force religion on his children from a very young age. I remember when I was about seven years old, when he very firmly told me, "Now don't come out of your bedroom until you can recite the "Our Father" and "Hail Mary." Then he left and closed the door behind him. Dad's hypocrisy is what has kept my brother Michael from following God or becoming a member of any church. Michael observed Dad going to church and praying a rote prayer of thanks at the dinner table, but also observed Dad behaving like the devil himself.

My father's evil behaviors only convinced Michael that there can't possibly be a God. If there is a God, he doesn't want to have anything to do with a God who allows such suffering as Michael not only experienced, but also observed in our mother.

I had my first real experience with Jesus the summer following my junior year. I heard about a weekend retreat for teens called Search. I don't know what made me go because my father didn't make me do it, and I knew not one person who was going. Grace maybe? Nana's prayers? This retreat weekend was a life-changing experience for me. I was like a sponge soaking up everything they had to offer. I not only benefited from the things that I heard, but I was an active participant and shared my thoughts and feelings willingly with the entire group.

There were two moments that really touched me and have stuck with me over all these years. The leaders played an audio dramatization of the crucifixion of Jesus. While listening, I had my eyes closed, but as I heard the nails being hammered into Jesus' hands, I could see it in my mind's eye. It was as if I was right there two thousand years ago when it happened. I was filled with such compassion, I began to sob.

The other moment came shortly after, when they asked us to imagine Jesus walking into the room. I immediately dropped my head to the floor in shame and humility, trying to hide my face from Jesus. All I could think of was that I wasn't worthy to be in His presence. That moment caused me to be sorry for my sins and led me to repent to my Savior.

Life following the retreat was different for me and my family. I started to behave differently with my father. If he was mean to me by yelling at me, or being unfair to me, I didn't yell back. I stopped reacting to my father. I seemed to have a steady peace about me, and greater love. I started getting up early to pray each day.

Because of the changes my father saw in me, he decided to file for an annulment so that he would be right with the Catholic Church. He also wanted to renew his vows with Donna, and to do so in the church. It was a blessed occasion a few years later when I got to sing the song "The Blessing of Aaron" at their wedding ceremony. Within time, my father started to change. He became nicer to me; gentler and more loving. He became affectionate, in the pure sense of the word. He started to listen to me, and to truly respect my opinion. During the two years or so that it lasted, life was bliss between Dad and me.

My senior year was the "happy year." I had never been happier. I had Jesus in my heart, and Dad and I were getting along. School that year was fun and exciting. Highlights of my senior year included spending most of the school day in the Art wing. This is where I developed the majority of the art skills I possess today. At the end of the school year I won the Art award at the Senior Awards Dinner.

I also sang in the annual variety show. This year's experience was better than the last. My Uncle Scott was doing his teaching internship at my school that year, and was a member of a band playing bass guitar on weekends. I approached my talented and hip uncle and asked if he would accompany me on guitar along with Bonnie, and he accepted. Uncle Scott, Bonnie and I had such fun rehearsing Linda Ronstadt's version of "Desperado." They each played and sang background vocals. The night of the show was magical!

During our senior year Bonnie and I spent most of our weekends together and we had such fun. To top it all off, on graduation day my parents threw me a huge party where family and friends gathered. For the first time I felt that my parents were proud of me. I felt so special that day.

There is no other way to describe what happened following graduation except that maybe it was the devil's plan to deter me from the path that I was on, which included God and His righteousness. I don't like to even think about what happened next. I decided to go live with my mother in Florida. I thought there would be more opportunities there for a career. Also, I hadn't lived with my mother since I was twelve and wanted to give it a try.

I did visit Mom every summer during high school and must admit it was always a negative experience for me. The environment there continued to tempt me to behave immorally and illegally. For instance, I smoked pot, snorted cocaine, got drunk, hung out with older men and stayed out until late hours of the night.

Even though I was visiting Mom, I didn't see much of her. She still worked a lot, but now she spent her spare time with Carl with whom she married when I was fifteen. Every evening, my sister Elizabeth, my two step-sisters and I raised hell and partied on the town, while Mom and Carl kept to themselves behind closed doors.

Off I went, back to Florida at the age of seventeen. I didn't go off to college because I never once heard either of my parents suggest college to me. Once there, I got a job, went for voice lessons several times a week, went dancing with girl friends in night clubs, and dated guys—lots of them.

One day I met an older man who was quite gorgeous and he asked me out for a date. He picked me up at my house and we went out. This man took me to his house, led me to his bedroom, to his bed, and in the next moment, my virginity was gone. I hate to think of this moment. I was so tired of fighting off the nagging boys (or men) for so many years that I just gave in. I didn't want to do it. I didn't enjoy it. Deep down, I felt like a filthy rag. I don't remember the man's name, and I never saw him again. Later, I would come to realize why I let this man, and so many others use me. I had been made to believe that this was what I was good for. And this belief started with my father at a very young age.

My time in Florida became a temporary circumstance. Within the six months that I lived there I went from job to job, man to man; never finding a true friend that I could trust. As a matter of fact, in all of the years I spent in Florida, I was never to make a true friend. Every girlfriend I ever thought I could trust stabbed me in the back. This is why later in life I found it hard to trust in women, as well as men. As December rolled around, I went back to Portsmouth for Christmas vacation, and once there, decided that I didn't want to return to Florida.

Finally, a smart decision!

When I returned to my father's house everything was different. Dad was so happy to have me back that he stopped putting restrictions on me. He even stopped making me go to church. I guess he got attached to me over those years that I lived with him. I decided I was going to attend college. I got a taste of what it was like to be out there in the work force without a degree. The jobs I had in Florida left me empty. They seemed meaningless and shallow. I wanted to do something that would make a difference in the world.

I applied at the local community college as a music major, with voice as my main instrument. Dad didn't offer to help me out, so I applied for financial aid and got myself some employment. I made the decision to work for myself by cleaning homes. I put an ad in the paper and one thing led to another. Within no time, I had a decent clientele who paid me very well.

I continued to live the party life, which included picking up or being picked up by lots of men. There were a few times when I dated two men in the same day, one in the day and one in the night. After a few months of this, I started to think about going to church. Maybe I was feeling ashamed because of the choices that I was making regarding men. I made up my mind to go on a certain Sunday. I sat in the back of our local Catholic Church, and as I did, it was a new experience. The words I was hearing were coming to life within me. I was feeling something that I had never felt in all the days I attended church prior to that day.

I started to attend church faithfully every Sunday. On one of those Sundays I heard about a new campaign called "Renew." It involved small groups and a curriculum that was meant to help renew your faith. All I knew is that I wanted to get to know God in a deeper way, so I signed up. I attended Renew faithfully for the months that they offered it and I loved it. I met wonderful Christian people who became a support for me, and I grew closer to God, as I had wished. I became an active member of my church. My activities included leading a Renew group for the youth, singing in the youth choir, teaching children's Sunday school, lectoring and cantering. Every day I woke at 5:00 a.m. to pray and read the Bible before heading to college for my 8:00 a.m. class forty-five minutes away.

Peace and joy started to fill my soul.

Within a year, at the age of nineteen, a change came. For two years my father was a kinder man and our relationship was pretty good. But at this time, I began to notice a change in my father and it wasn't good. It was as if he was reverting back to his old ways. It got to the point when I felt that I wasn't going to stay around and witness his mean and abusive ways.

I spoke with one of my customers, an elderly man who owned a boarding house by the beach. He agreed to let me live and board with him, and my cleaning services would be accepted in lieu of paying rent. It was the perfect arrangement for me. I did have a need however, to make more money to pay for all of my other expenses. I got an additional job working weekends as a cocktail waitress at a night club. The money was great, the hours good, and I found it to be easy work. The negative aspect was that I was in the middle of the party scene—men, booze and drugs.

After a year of college, I felt I needed to drop out, due to lack of money. I needed to work more hours. Slowly over time I grew distant from God, and eventually stopped going to church. I did make more money as I had planned, but I was living deep in sin.

Bonnie and I became roommates and lived in Fall River, Massachusetts where the rent was cheaper. Bonnie was very motivated and had goals. At the end of a year, she applied to the University of Rhode Island and moved to an apartment close to school. Right around the same time, I got a job cocktail waitressing in a night club in Providence. I also decided it was time to go back to college, so I applied to Rhode Island College, also located in Providence. I found myself an apartment with two bedrooms near the college, and found a roommate through an ad I placed in the newspaper.

So after two decades, I ended up where it all started—where I started. Was it *divine providence*? Probably. It was there that I gave my heart to Jesus for the third time, and this time was "for keeps."

Chapter Three

Sometime later during prayer, this Croatian woman who is sitting beside me gets up to leave. But she hesitates. She turns around and reaches out her hand to take my hand. I put my hand in hers, as she proceeds to speak to me in perfect English, without even an accent! She says many things to me, but the gist of her message is, "God loves you very much. He treasures you. You are beautiful in His eyes...Do not marry anyone who doesn't feel the same way." Then she lets go of my hand, turns around and walks away.

It was 1988 when I entered Rhode Island College at the age of twenty-two. I was making enough money at a local night club to not have to work a second job. It wasn't all hard-earned money however, because I succumbed to peer-pressure from the other employees to skim money from the top. There was pressure to do as they were doing because they feared co-workers might turn them into the authorities. It's amazing how rampart the stealing ran, with the bartenders, as well as the waitresses.

I know that I have no excuse for stealing money the way I did. This goes to show you how lost I was, and that loyalty and honesty meant little to me. It is true that I knew right from wrong, but I feel that I might've chosen the right path had I been raised and molded to live an honest, moral life. What were my parents' values? How did they help instill in me a sense of righteousness and a desire to do what is good? I learned from them that I had to do whatever I could on my own to survive in the world and for me that meant taking the easy road whenever I saw the opportunity.

The good news is that ten years later, when married and walking with the Lord, I sent a check and letter to the company that I stole from. Repentance is great, but going a step further and offering restitution is even better. My conscience felt clean. What a great feeling!

At this time I broke my record for dating a man for more than a few months. I went steady with Doug for an entire year. This was a huge feat for me because whenever I started to fall in love with a man, or he with me, I *ran*! The term "to fall in love" usually gives a person a warm, fuzzy feeling. Well, not for me! That term was like hearing nails scratch the length of a chalkboard. It immediately conjured up feelings of fear.

I remember another man whom I dated prior to Doug. He was kind and loving towards me, and we had such a wonderful time together. One day, after spending the entire weekend together, which was glorious, I had a meltdown. While in his presence I started to sob. I didn't know why I was crying; I just knew I had to get away from him. As he was trying to comfort me and understand why I was crying, I pushed him away from me and left his house. I made sure I never again saw this man.

I had a bad habit with men. When things started to get deep, I would act very mean towards them. This was my way of keeping them at arm's length. I didn't want to feel. Feelings were not good. They always led to pain. One could say I was abusive towards men, in the verbal sense. The kinder the man, the more I wanted to push him away. I remember doing this with Doug.

I can remember the exact moment when he told me he loved me for the first time. As he spoke this to my face, I started to cry, and then physically pushed him away from me. I hated hearing those words. And then he said that I was beautiful. My thoughts were that he couldn't possibly feel that way because I knew it wasn't true. For some reason I stayed with Doug. He was a nice companion to have and he helped to keep loneliness at bay. Doug and I spoke about spending a lifetime together. We spoke of the details, but I soon realized that he wasn't the one for me.

Once, while shopping in a local store, my eyes fell on a magazine. On the cover was a woman in the most beautiful wedding gown I ever saw. It was magical. I bought the magazine, which is something that I never did, just to gaze at the photo of the dress. I loved the way it made me feel when I looked at it. Within a few weeks, I was browsing the mall while

Christmas shopping, and spotted the same dress that was on my magazine cover. A week later, I went back to the bridal store and tried on the dress. As I looked at myself in the mirror, I knew I wasn't going to wear a wedding dress with Doug.

I took Bonnie back to the store so she could see the dress. Her first words as I modeled the dress were, "Holly, *that* is you!" I tried it on a third time for another friend of mine, and he had the same response as Bonnie. I made up my mind at that moment. I was going to buy the dress. It took me a full year of monthly payments to pay for it. After I got it, I paid a store to professionally store it so that it would be safe and preserved. All this and I was a struggling college student trying to make ends meet. I guess it made me hope—hope for the happy ending, like Cinderella. I wanted that. Bonnie had a full hope chest that her mother helped her fill. I had my hope dress.

Bonnie has continued to be a support for me through the years. If it weren't for Bonnie I might not have received my college diploma. There was a time when I just didn't think I had it in me to complete my studies and get a degree. Bonnie wouldn't hear of it. She told me I was talking nonsense and that I could do it. Her believing in me made all the difference. She and Auntie both spurred me on to achieve this goal, and I am truly grateful.

I'll never forget graduation day when I received my bachelor's degree. This day is one of the highlights of my life. Rhode Island was in the midst of a heat wave and our ceremony was midday under the merciless hot rays of the sun. The outfit that I chose to wear that day was especially memorable—a bathing suit! Well—it was hidden under my graduation gown. I thought it was a clever idea, born out of all the education I had received.

Following the ceremony, family members and friends gathered at my apartment for a fun-filled, albeit sweltering hot celebration. My pastor Fr. Randall even came. All of my favorite people were there, including my Nana and my Auntie. My most memorable present that day came from Bonnie. I opened up a gift to a beautiful opal ring with diamond chips. I was so overcome with joy and humility that she would think so much of me as to buy me such a beautiful gift. I guess it was her way of showing me that she was proud of my accomplishment. Few people in my life showed that they treasured me. This is the reason why I cherish this memory, even after all these years.

My apartment near college was only minutes from my old neighborhood where Auntie still lived. Once a week I went to Auntie's for dinner, and never did I leave empty-handed. She loved to send me home with a bag full of food, including her homemade goodies. Auntie spent time during the winter months teaching me to sew so that I was able to have affordable gifts for my family during the holidays. She also shared her recipes and showed me how to cook and bake. As we worked side by side, she passed along her childhood stories, and thus the wisdom she obtained through them. Once again, Auntie cared for me as a mother would.

Right around the time I broke it off with Doug, I bumped into an old neighbor from Portsmouth. She told me about a prayer meeting that she was facilitating at my old church. She invited me to go and within a week, I decided I would. I believe that I was empty inside and tired of trying to find happiness, but getting nowhere. *"Why not turn back to God?"* I thought. *"Yes, this is exactly what I need."*

Before I speak of what happened next, I'd like to speak of Holly—before Christ; before the transformation—for God has done an incredible work in me! If you knew me then, you might have thought of me as an intimidating person. I learned that tactic from my father. This was my way of keeping people in their place, and to make them fear doing anything to hurt me.

I also flirted a lot with men. I loved the attention I received, and all of their words of flattery. On the other hand, I was cold and stand-offish to women. I didn't trust women, hence, I didn't think it was possible to have a woman as a friend. Whenever I started to get close to a female friend, I severed the relationship by either being inaccessible, or hurting them with my words. This would make them distance themselves from me. I could be very harsh, for I chose not to empathize with others. That only meant that I had to have feelings for them.

At the same time, I empathized to a great deal with the weak, underprivileged, handicapped, and victims of abuse. This embodied a group of people who were weaker than me, thus, they had no ability to control or hurt me. This aspect of my personality, as you will learn, drew me to protect the unborn, support unwed mothers, assist the underprivileged; befriend ill, handicapped, and foster children—all children in general.

Other undesirable traits included being controlling and manipulative. These I learned became my survival tactics. If I could control everyone and everything around me, so as to keep all persons from hurting me, and all unpredictable occurrences from occurring, I would be safe. Everything would be OK. You probably wouldn't have liked me B.C. (before Christ). I've had people tell me that they didn't like me and only came to like me after they saw the transformation that God worked in me.

I remember the first prayer meeting I attended. It was *all* good! I loved the people I met. They exuded the joy and love of God. They welcomed me and made me feel as if I belonged. The next part of my story is going to get my readers excited. There will be some buzzing amongst my friends of today who are non-Catholics. It will be controversial, but I swear to tell the truth; the truth as I understand it to be.

The truth is that a major conversion of heart happened in me while I was visiting a place called Medjugorje, Yugoslavia, now known as Bosnia Hercegovenia, where there are reported apparitions of the Blessed Mother of God.

On my first visit to this prayer meeting, four of the members were talking about a trip to Medjugorje that they would be going on. I had seen a documentary on PBS about this phenomenon, so I knew a little about it. I went home that evening and started to think about going.

Since 1984, it is said that the Mother of Jesus has been appearing to six young people on a daily basis. Her first words were "I have come to tell you that God exists." She gives messages to the (originally children, but are now adults) six visionaries that are meant for the world. She advises us to pray, fast, read the Bible, and confess our sins. She expresses her desire for God's children to have peace, and that in order to have peace in our world, we must first have peace in our hearts, and then in our families.

I took this decision to prayer, whether I should travel on this pilgrimage with my new friends. I found out how much it would cost me for the trip and lo and behold, I had the exact amount in my savings account. The only drawback is that upon the return of my trip, I would have nothing left in my account, and no job because I had just left my job as a cocktail waitress. It was a scary thought not to know where my future provisions would come from, so I definitely felt that I needed God's blessing in my decision. After praying about it, I decided to put my faith in God that He would take care of my needs upon my return.

My trip was a major life-changing event. Within a few days, my friends observed a change in me; in my disposition. They told me that I was warmer; more loving and kinder. They also commented at how peaceful I appeared. While there, I felt God's peace within me—a peace that I had never felt before.

I also witnessed miracles while there. There was one incident that occurred that has affected my life for the better. I was in church praying with the entire congregation and sitting between my friend Pete and a Croatian woman whom I didn't know. I knew the woman was Croatian because you could tell the village women apart from foreign women, and also, when she prayed, she spoke in a different language. This woman got up to leave, but before she did, she spoke to me. I must include how she appeared as she spoke to me. Her face was radiant and exuded joy, and her eyes looked right into my soul. I swear that I was visited by an angel.

The moment she walked away, I was dumbfounded. I immediately started to sob with the acknowledgment of what the woman had said to me.

The words of God were hitting home to me. I became overwhelmed by the knowledge that God loved *me*. Afterwards, I asked Pete if he heard what the woman said, and he replied that he didn't. He did say however, "I saw her face though, and it radiated. There was a glow to her." That was confirmation for me. God sent an angel to speak to me! A year later, God would remind me of these words, and it would change my life.

Another life-changing incident that occurred while on this pilgrimage has to do with repentance. During all hours of the day, priests sit inside and outside of the church to hear confessions. There are numerous priests from various countries who sit for hours and hear the confessions of hundreds of people who wait in long lines to repent of their sins. I followed my friends and stood in line. I must have waited in my line for at least an hour and as I did, I examined my conscience. Every time I thought of a "really bad" sin, I thought, "*Oh no, I can't tell that one.*"

But when it was my time to confess to the priest, out came the things that I vowed I wouldn't say…the stealing, the sleeping around, and so on. I was reduced to sobbing. I walked away from the priest still in tears. I continued to sob throughout the entire evening prayer service. I just couldn't stop the tears. What a joyous relief I felt.

Overall, what most affected me on this trip was a feeling. I had this feeling that God loved me. I felt the love of a father; of God the Father. It felt good. It felt warm. I felt embraced and cared for. This was enough to change me—my life, my actions, my desires, my interests—forever. I use the scripture from John 6:68 to describe how I felt at this time. Many of Jesus' followers were leaving Him because His words were too hard for them to accept. Jesus asked His disciples if they were going to leave as well. Peter tells Jesus, "To whom shall we go? You have the words of everlasting life." After experiencing the love of God, there was no one else I wanted to be with, and nowhere else that I wanted to be, other than by Jesus' side—forever.

When I returned back to Providence from my trip I was a different person. I began living a different life. I quit smoking pot and drinking alcohol, quit using curse words, and quit hanging out with anyone whom I felt was living an immoral life. I began praying on a daily basis, fasting on bread and water on Fridays, going to church regularly, attending weekly prayer meetings, and periodically, a weekend retreat. I was thirsty for God. I was a sponge soaking Him in as much as I could. Before school, I would get up every morning and pray for at least an hour. I would sit and listen to God, sing worship songs, or read the Bible.

One memorable day, as I sat at my kitchen table, my roommate came in the door. She brought with her a friend from college of whom I had never met. She introduced us and then they left the room. Within five minutes my roommate's friend left. I thought, *"Well that was a short visit."* My roommate then came to me to tell me that her friend who was a self-professed witch ("a good witch") said that she saw angels all over our house. It sort of freaked my roommate out, but I was glad. I'd rather have angels living with me than devils!

A year and a half after my first trip, I returned to Medjugorje for Christmas of 1990. It was the most blessed Christmas I have ever had. It was the simplest Christmas because the complete focus was on Christ. The villagers were so poor that they couldn't afford Christmas trees, lights, decorations, or store-bought presents. We pilgrims didn't have our family or friends, malls to shop in, cars to drive, or money to spend. We just had each other and our faith. That Christmas was sweet. It was precious.

On this trip I didn't see many miracles with my eyes, although my group of twenty did see a supernatural vision while in town one day. I stayed back at our residence, only to hear of this Christmas miracle. Many, many villagers saw the same image. They saw at a distance, a white silhouette of what appeared to be Mary holding baby Jesus, and Joseph walking beside. They appeared to be traveling up one of the hillsides in the village. My friend took a photo of it, and there it is, captured on paper.

During this trip God began a new work in me. It had to do with suffering. My first trip had to do with the knowledge that God loved me. On this trip, almost everything that occurred to me or in me had to do with relating to the suffering of Jesus Christ.

One evening as my friends and I walked by the light of our flashlights up one of the small mountains, I was startled by something I saw. As I looked down to take a step on the path made of stones, I saw a vision of the head of Christ. He wore the crown of thorns and his face displayed an agonizing pain. Another person in my group of five saw it also. We both jumped back and shrieked simultaneously. This vision only lasted a moment. I then took a picture of the stone. One can see in the picture that it resembles the crowned-head of Jesus. But the picture only reveals a natural stone, and does not capture the supernatural picture or vision that my friend and I experienced in that first gaze.

On another day my friend Mike asked me to climb another mountain in the village which leads to the top where people pray and feel close to God. On the way up the hill are the Stations of the Cross, where one is reminded through icons of all of the significant moments when Jesus suffered in His last days.

As I traveled up this small mountain, it was as if I was walking with Jesus on the road to Calvary. The thoughts became so real to me. It was as if I could feel some of the pain that Jesus felt. The reason why it is important for me to share the times when God brought me close to the suffering of Christ is because I believe that He was preparing me for the suffering that He knew I was to endure in the near future.

Let me tell you of another amazing conversion which happened through Medjugorje, of a man named Joe. When I met Joe he was already a priest, but he told me exactly how that came to be. He started out as a broker on Wall Street, making six figures. The change came after a trip with friends to tour Europe. One of his friends wanted to stop at Medjugorje, so the rest of the group followed along. When it was time for them to leave Medjugorje, Joe stayed behind. He stayed there for an entire month, never again to return to Wall Street. While he was there he felt God calling him to the priesthood. When he returned to the States, he sold everything he had and joined a seminary.

Joe chose a religious order that chooses to live a life of poverty exactly the way that St. Francis of Assisi lived; with no possessions and no money. They possess only one cloak and a single pair of sandals, which they wear when walking the streets to share the Gospel of Christ with those they meet. They offer to work for their food without formal employment, or they beg for it, as St. Francis did.

I was amazed by Joe's story. It reminds me of the rich man who met Jesus and asked what else he could do besides follow the Ten Commandments. Jesus told him to sell everything he had and to follow him. The man walked away sad because he had a lot of possessions. Jesus replied in Matthew 19:24, "It is easier for a camel to pass through the eye of a needle than for a rich man to enter the kingdom of heaven."

Regarding the topic of trusting in God for our provisions, I wish to testify to the fact that each time I returned from a trip and was unemployed, God was faithful and cared for all of my needs. Before my second trip, I had asked my employer to give me the week off and he replied that he couldn't allow it. Again I took the decision to prayer and found my answer by means of a small miracle. As I was entering a chapel to pray, I began small talk with a woman who was just leaving. In our conversation, we spoke of Medjugorje. I then explained my dilemma and that is when she stopped mid-sentence, to tell me that she saw a vision of a hand that was giving me a blessing upon my forehead. She also spoke words that meant that I was to take the trip.

For a second time, I found myself in need and sought God to provide. My financial needs where great. I was a full-time college student and had to pay for all of my own expenses. I had to pay my rent and a car payment, in addition to needing money for food and clothes. As I spent time looking for employment, money just seemed to fall into my lap. I had an aunt who for no apparent reason, and was known to be stingy, give me a check for three hundred dollars. I also had friends even younger than I, give me money.

One time while at my church's prayer meeting, the pastor, unbeknownst to me, passed his hat around and collected money to give to me. That same pastor, weeks later, came to me with an envelope that was collected during the Sunday service offering. He gave me a sealed envelope that read, "To the girl who spent all of her money to go to Medjugorje." The envelope contained a lone one hundred dollar bill. It was so special to me that I didn't want to spend it. Instead, I placed this gift from my Father in my Bible.

There is another moment that is memorable to me, where God clearly had worked behind the scenes and sent me provisions. One day I happened to be in a Christian book store, when the owner whom I knew as a friend, approached me. She told me that there was a woman, Ms. Podvin, who was also in the store and was looking to pay someone to drive her to see her daughter who lived an hour away at college. I was told she would give me fifty dollars. I agreed to drive her.

On the morning that I was to pick up Ms. Podvin, God spoke to me in prayer. He gave me the scripture verse from Matthew 6:25-33, which reads,

> "Do not worry about your life, what you are to eat or drink...Look at the birds of the air, they do not sow or reap, and yet your heavenly Father feeds them...Why do you worry about your clothes? See how the flowers of the field grow...Yet I tell you that not even Solomon in all his splendor was dressed like one of these...Seek first His kingdom and His righteousness and all of these things will be given to you."

By the end of the day, God brought this promise to fruition.

When we arrived to pick up Ms. Podvin's daughter, I was invited to eat dinner with them. A free dinner in a decent restaurant was quite a treat for me, being a struggling college student! I got along well with Ms. Podvin's daughter who was close in age, and I got to share my faith with her as well, so it was an enjoyable afternoon. The blessings didn't end there however.

Upon our return, Ms. Podvin insisted on me going in when I dropped her off. Once inside, I discovered that her house was like a store. Along the walls stood shelves of brand new items, much of which were Christian articles. She kept taking things off the shelves such as books, jewelry, and stuffed animals and handing them to me. She then went into her kitchen cupboards and began filling bags for me with food. At the end of the day, I entered my apartment with my arms full. As I emptied my bags to find room on my shelves, I was brought back to the scripture that God had given me that morning..."And all of these things will be added unto you." God's promises are true!

I realize that my non-Catholic friends might be filled with many opposing thoughts about the mother of God appearing on this earth. I am simply telling things as they have happened in my life. Considering this controversial subject, I wish to point out a particular scripture found in Matthew 7:16-18, "By their fruit you will recognize them. A bad tree cannot bear good fruit." Through the events in Medjugorje, I have only seen people's lives change for the good. Twenty years later, I see my friends who traveled to Medjugorje, and like me, they are still walking closely with God and devote their lives to Christian ministries.

Following my conversion I sought out a church to attend. A neighbor and college friend of mine invited me to his church which was called St. Charles Borromeo Church. From the first day I attended, I knew I belonged there. Pastor Fr. John Randall and the congregation were on fire for the Lord, just as I felt I was. Fr. Randall was a very popular person throughout the US due to his involvement and promotion of the Charismatic Movement (also known as the Catholic Pentecostal Movement) on the East Coast. Fr. Randall was so popular that members drove an hour to hear his sermons, thus the reason why it was considered a "commuter's parish."

The Sunday service lasted an hour and a half, yet no one hurried to the door to leave. It began with a standing ovation to God, followed by a half hour of praise and worship music, which accompanied clapping hands and hands rose in exultation. Father's sermons lasted at least a half hour, but left you wanting more. If you entered the church on any given Sunday, you would see the physically handicapped, the mentally challenged, the homeless, and people of all walks of life. Everyone felt welcomed. Everyone belonged.

There was a large following at daily mass, in which I attended for most of the seven years I was a member. Fr. Randall held a Charismatic prayer meeting every Thursday evening which held three hundred members. Fr. Randall preached often about the importance of having the Holy Spirit in one's life and of being soaked in the knowledge of God's Word. Father held Life in the Spirit seminars year round so that people could learn about and be baptized in the Holy Spirit (Matthew 3:10-12). I had already gone through this seminar at my last place of worship, and it was there that I was baptized in the Holy Spirit.

Father also held groups year round where one could learn about God's Word. Father founded the radio talk show, "The Spirit and the Word," which was just one of the church's many ministries. Another extensive ministry is called St. Vincent De Paul, a ministry for the poor. Since the church is located in the inner city of Providence there is a great need in the local community.

I attribute the foundation of my faith to St. Charles. I often viewed St. Charles as a school, but also as a hospital, in the spirit sense. I observed that many of the church members grew a strong foundation in the Word, as well as in the Spirit, and after several years moved on to their local church community. I also observed how God brought many members to their wounded pasts, and guided them through the healing process to wholeness and happiness. When the Holy Spirit is present, so are His power, mercy, and the desire to bring healing. It happened to me, and to so many other people, many of whom were my friends. Inner healings and physical healings were not a rare occurrence at St. Charles.

All of the good generated at St. Charles I attribute to the leadership of Fr. Randall. Fr. Randall was a well-loved and holy man of God, known to never forget a name. If you met him, you would feel that he was interested in you and what you had to say. He would make you feel important, no matter whom you were or what position you held. He was an excellent preacher, known to grab your attention with the liveliness of his sermons. He was known, while preaching, to leap across the platform, throw a book through the air, jump up and down, and whisper and shout. He was a doer of the Word and full of wisdom and deep concern for his church members.

Father was shepherd of the St. Charles community for twenty-three years, until he retired. Following retirement, he wrote one last book that sums up his years in the Lord. In addition to several other books he wrote, his most recent was entitled, *No Spirit-No Church.*

I am personally grateful to Fr. Randall for taking me under his wing and being like a father to me. He guided me, nurtured me, and expressed his concern for me. He mentored me and my fiancé as we prepared for marriage, and then con-celebrated at our marriage ceremony.

Fr. Randall was only one of the father figures that I've had in my life. I feel that over the years God has put men in my life that would stand in His place. There have been times that, without a doubt, I felt God's fatherly love pour through these father figures. At the beginning of my walk with the Lord in 1989, I met Bob (an older man) at my first prayer meeting. He was the first man I ever admired. We became close friends over the years, but he was also a mentor to me. He guided me spiritually, as well as in other areas of my life. Knowing Bob made me hope that I could meet a man like him, one who is kind and wouldn't hurt me. I had never desired to marry a man until meeting Bob.

I soon came to find another father figure in my pastor at St. Augustine's Church. There is much bad talk of Catholic priests in today's society, but I know of three who were righteous, God-fearing, and holy men of God. These men modeled the love of God the Father to me. Monsignor Egan, now deceased, became my second father figure. He was actually the same age as my grandfather. Nevertheless, he was there for me as a loving, biological father would be to her daughter.

God knew the history with my father, and He graciously was restoring me and bringing healing to me through these father figures. Every time Msgr. Egan and I met, when he would give me spiritual guidance and hear my confession, he would slip me a twenty dollar bill, just as a father would. As I moved on to become a member of St. Charles, Fr. Randall stepped into the father-figure role.

My fourth father figure was Father Hugh. I used to attend an inner-city mission which was open day and night. At this Franciscan mission, priests heard the confessions of people for hours each day. This is how I met Fr. Hugh. Fr. Hugh (also the age of my grandfather) and I clicked. There was something special about him, and he felt the same about me.

I met with Fr. Hugh every month for about eleven years until he retired and moved back to his home state of New Jersey. I would meet with him for spiritual direction and confession. But we also conversed as friends would. In the beginning when I was single and struggling financially, he would slip me money just as Msgr. Egan did. Father would find creative ways of slipping money to me which he meant to be of assistance to me, to lighten my load. Once he gave me a coffee mug in a box which had a twenty dollar bill hidden inside.

Fr. Hugh and I shared a love for poetry and art, as well as our Lord. He encouraged me with the things that I was good at. He praised me and gave me compliments which helped to build up my self-esteem. He had a way of lifting me up. After I married and had children, Father became like a family member.

As Father was approaching old age and dealing with health problems, I was there to comfort, assist, and lift *him* up. I found myself praying at his hospital bedside on more than one occasion. Just thinking about Fr. Hugh makes my eyes well up with tears. I miss him very much. Once he retired and moved to New Jersey to live with his brother, I never heard from him again. He was dealing with dementia at that point, and technically I wasn't family; but I felt like I was. In my heart he was my family. He was the father I never had. He's probably in heaven at this moment and I can't wait to be reunited with him there.

Chapter Four

I am walking down the hall of the children's ward on my way to the play room when I spot him. He is sitting there with his little deformed body, staring every which way, with drool dripping from his lips and a tube jutting from his throat. I abruptly turn my head the other way in an effort to forget what I had just seen, as if to pretend the boy with a name isn't there at all.

While still in Providence and attending college, I decided I wanted to spend time with children at the hospital. I went with the intention of putting smiles on the children's faces. In retrospect, I wonder if the reason why I sought to comfort sick children stems from wanting to comfort and soothe the wounded child within. I visited the Child Life Department at Rhode Island Hospital and met with the director. We agreed that I would spend my Saturday mornings with the children because that was the day when there was no staff on duty. It was there that I met Nicky.

The last time I saw Nicky was in 1991, twenty years ago. It was a long time ago, but I haven't forgotten him. The memories I have of him are so rich and fresh in my mind. Nicky was born with severe

Cerebral Palsy. He was also born blind. He lived all of his five years in either the hospital or a hospital-like building for severely ill children. His family rarely ever visited him. They stayed away from Nicky, as was my first reaction. Children like him are not very attractive and the extent of their handicaps can be frightening. For months I passed by the severely handicapped children who sat like statues in the hall, until one day I took a turn into Nicky's room.

    I remember that first day vividly. I walked over to the window next to his bed and pulled up the blinds. When I did so, the sun hit Nicky's face and I captured a sudden move of his lips that formed a smile. Later I told the nurses that Nicky had smiled when I pulled up the blinds, but they said that it was just a muscle reflex. I didn't know whether to believe them or not. However, I would soon find out that Nicky did indeed smile! As I got to know him over subsequent visits, I discovered that Nicky could communicate with me. Most of those visits he let me know how happy I made him.

    Nicky always smiled when I sang him songs or whistled tunes, as poor as they sounded to me! Nicky often had the tip of his tongue sitting on his bottom lip. One day I tapped it, and he immediately stuck it back in his mouth and then smiled. He continued to stick it out as in a game, and I continued to tap it. He enjoyed this little game. The next time I visited him; I walked in and said a few words to the nurse attending him. Immediately Nicky stuck his tongue out with a smile. I realized then that he knew who I was. I also came to learn that Nicky enjoyed being tickled, as any five year old would. When I tickled him, he would scrunch his body up, and display a huge smile across his face.

I have a very significant memory of Nicky which at the time brought tears to my eyes. Every time I think of this moment, the tears start flowing. On a particular visit, I sat down beside Nicky in his bed. Nicky's arms and legs, feet and hands, were curled up, and stiff, which is usual for a person with Cerebral Palsy. As I sang him songs, I gently massaged the arm and leg which were closest to me. I started at his shoulder and worked my way down to his toes. As I did this, his limbs slowly straightened out, and became relaxed and flexible.

Before my eyes it was as if a miracle had occurred. The side of the body that I attended to was completely straight, which I had never seen before, and the other side was still curled up. The physical therapists had stopped working with him because his family decided that the time was coming when they would discontinue keeping him alive by false means. Nicky simply lay in bed all day with no stimulation whatsoever, except for the occasional visit to sit in the hall.

On the same floor as Nicky was a boy named James, who also had Cerebral Palsy. He was sixteen years old and in the hospital because he was being prepared to receive braces on his legs so that he could walk. James was treated with such love and care from his parents. He was never left alone in the hospital. I got to know this family over several weeks time.

When James was born the doctors gave his parents such little hope. They said that he would never even sit up. His parents behaved as if they never heard those lousy, discouraging words about their son. James' father started a business where he could work from the home, so that he could assist in the care of James. His mother became a stay-at-home mom. They also had a daughter. This family treated James with expectancy and hope. They showered him with love, and in many ways, treated him as if he had no limitations.

It was very evident to me that James was happy and thriving, and improving, due to the love and attention his parents gave him. Thanks to them, James was being schooled. And he was now going to receive braces and learn to walk. James' life was treated as invaluable, whereas Nicky was treated as if he wasn't alive. I discovered that Nicky was very much alive. Unfortunately, I would soon learn that Nicky's life was going to be taken away from him. One day when I came to the hospital; I walked into Nicky's room to find that he was no longer there. The nurses said that he had been taken back to the place where he was living before, to die "comfortably." His parents decided to pull the feeding tube and let him die "a natural death."

I found out where the building was and visited Nicky there. No one ever questioned who I was or what I was doing there. I was the only one who visited Nicky and I figured that the nurses felt my visits couldn't hurt him. The first time I visited him, he was in a crib and not looking well. He was literally starving to death. My first instinct was to pray with him, but I was told before I began volunteering not to mention God or pray with the children.

My second visit with Nicky at this building brought about another miracle. Nicky on this day was in a small cradle that sat on the floor. His body was quite small now. I sat down beside his cradle at eye level and began to sing songs about Jesus. He had never looked me in the eye as a person with eye sight would, but on this day he had a particular look in his eyes.

As I sang my heart out to Nicky, he appeared to be listening intently, and had a dreamy look in his eyes. He seemed mesmerized by my singing, and filled with peace. Each time I began to sing another song he would appear with a wide smile, as if to say, *"Oh good! Another one!"* Once again, I had tears rolling down my face and I felt joy. I knew I was bringing him joy at that moment.

Several days later, while at home, I started to think of Nicky. For the first time ever, I decided to call to see how he was. When I called, a nurse told me that they expected him to pass on at any time. I immediately got into my car and went to visit Nicky.

When I arrived at Nicky's room, a nurse was rocking him in her arms. He had a pasty blue color to his skin.

I didn't stay too long because the nurse was with him. As I walked out of Nicky's room, another nurse spotted me. She told me that Nicky had been baptized, and received the Sacrament of the Anointing of the Sick. I left there grateful that someone had prayed with him and blessed him, and also grateful that the nurse had given me this information. She really had no reason to share it with me, considering I was of no relation to Nicky.

The next day I called to see how Nicky was doing and I was told that he passed on shortly after I had left. A few days later I entered a church. I knelt down to pray and began to think of Nicky's passing. I started to cry in sorrow. But suddenly I got a picture in my mind of Nicky skipping around and whistling as if he didn't have a care in the world. My sorrowful tears turned into joyful ones. I knew that Nicky was in the care of God, his Father, and all was good. I never cried another tear of sorrow for Nicky. Nicky is alive and happy. He is dancing and singing in the presence of God and all the angels.

Every year on July 3rd, the day Nicky passed on, I spend the day thinking of the special memories of him that I treasure in my heart. I always find someone that I can share his story with. I don't want the memory of him to ever fade away. What I learned from knowing Nicky has richly blessed my life. This experience with Nicky inspired me to write about it in an essay which was published by the Providence Journal.

After knowing Nicky, I decided to spend my time with the severely ill or handicapped children who were like him. There were many repeat patients in the hospital that had severe Cerebral Palsy. I found one of the things that always got a joyful response with these kids was to play instruments, no skill necessary. If I banged on a drum or dragged a mallet across a xylophone, I always got a smile and an enthusiastic posture.

I lived to see a smile on these kids faces. Because I was attracted to special needs kids so much, I left the hospital and began working at Meeting Street School, which is strictly for handicapped children. I assisted the art teacher who taught children of the age of three. I continued this job on Saturdays until I took a full time live-in position at a home for unwed mothers.

In 1991 following college graduation, I was contemplating what I might do for work. I was thinking about starting my own business where I would contract with schools and such, and apply the skills and knowledge I gained in college. However, I was feeling a tugging from our Lord. I felt that He was going to ask me to do something. I waited for His "call," and I knew that I was to be obedient and say "yes."

I did get a call. Literally. A woman who I had met a few days prior, called me and asked me if I wanted to work for her. The position was to be house manager at a home for unwed mothers called The Little Flower Home. I had never even heard of this home, yet I knew within my heart that I had to say yes. I had a burning inside my heart. I knew this was it—what I had been waiting for.

Sophia, the founder of this Christian home, told me that it was a live-in position so I couldn't bring any of my furniture. She also told me that I couldn't bring my cat. The home was a half hour away, located in the country, so it would be a distance from my circle of friends located in the city. All of the sacrifices I would have to make didn't make me hesitate to take this position being offered to me. I just knew I had to take it. This was the start of a year that was filled with a wealth of meaningful experiences. At the year's end, I felt that I had never learned as much in all of my years as I had in this one.

And I had my miracle stories to take with me.

The home could hold up to seven girls whose average age was fourteen. Some of the girls came from the streets and some had been drug users. Some had several abortions prior to coming to the home. About ninety-five percent of the girls had been molested or date-raped at some time in their life. When these girls came to the home, it was the lowest point in their lives. Because of their circumstances, the girls were usually depressed, unfriendly, and disagreeable. The burnout rate for house managers was about three months. Volunteers who offered their time and talents with the girls didn't last very long, due to the girls' negative attitudes and behaviors. Sometimes the volunteers didn't return a second time.

The home had only two members on staff, not including volunteers. The other house manager's name was Millie. I think very highly of Millie because of the way that she walks out her faith. She is a true image of Jesus Himself. From the moment Millie and I met in the warm country kitchen of the home, I knew we were kindred spirits. She offered me a cup of tea and her friendship quite readily. Millie was much older than me and filled with a wealth of knowledge.

Millie taught me what it meant to follow Jesus. She daily left her own desires behind so to give of herself to serve God and, in this case, the unwed mothers to whom she ministered. She not only served the girls, but also me, the volunteers, and everyone else that she met throughout the day. She was kind and gentle; and possessed mountain-moving faith. I looked up to her and tried to model her. I felt blessed to have her in my life as my friend, but also as a guide concerning my work in this ministry. Following our time at the home, Millie and I remained friends, and a decade later, she became the godmother of my third son Richard.

While working at the home, Millie and I made it a point to visit its small chapel for prayer. We knew that we had to cling to prayer in order to be refreshed by the Holy Spirit daily. We especially needed His grace to love these girls who tested our love on a daily basis. There is one girl named Barbara, who sticks out the most in my mind. She gave me the hardest time within that year. She acted as if she despised me from the day she entered the home. Barbara wouldn't even allow me to touch her. I regularly would lay my hands on the girls' bellies and pray for their child growing within, all except Barbara. After one evening where I had done this with a few of the girls, Barbara had quite an amazing story to tell on the following morning. At breakfast in the kitchen I found that she was telling a story about what she said had happened in the middle of the night.

"Holly came into my bedroom last night. She walked over to my bed, laid her hands on my belly and prayed." I was shocked to hear her say this.

"That is untrue. I don't recall doing that at all, and I've never been told that I sleep walk."

Barbara swore up and down that I did go into her room.

I argued, "Maybe you dreamed that I did."

"No. I know what I know. You came into my room."

Barbara convincingly stuck to her story. I think it was a "God" thing, a divine or supernatural experience.

This happened in the beginning of Barbara's stay. I am happy to say that after much suffering (wounded pride) and prayers, Barbara had come to love me and be my friend. It wasn't until close to the end of her stay at the home, but nevertheless, I got to see the grace of God transform this young lady and it was very rewarding. Barbara joined me in attending my church on Sundays and weekly prayer meetings. Near the end, Barbara went back to live with her mother. She invited me to her home several times, including the day of her son's baptism.

Another memorable story is about Laurel. One evening when she was four months along in her pregnancy, I laid my hands on her belly and prayed for her unborn baby. "It moved! My baby moved!" she exclaimed. It was the first time she had ever felt her baby move. It was a special moment. Laurel ended up leaving the home before delivering her baby, but after her baby arrived she called me. She told me that her baby had almost died upon delivery because he had the cord wrapped around his neck. She told me that her baby came through the trauma and was a healthy baby. "And I *know* that it was your prayers Holly that saved Julian." She thanked me and asked me to be the godmother of her baby.

I became godmother to Julian, in addition to my sister's children, Lee and Billy, Bonnie's daughter Kay, and another friend's son named Kent. Laurel, like Barbara, also joined me at my church every Sunday, and we became lasting friends.

My schedule at the home was four days on and three days off. However, I was still in the home seven days a week because it was a live-in position. The home was located in a former convent and shared the property with a church. The church was next door and had a small chapel that was open twenty-four hours a day. Every morning I went to pray alone in the chapel at 7:00 and then went to daily Mass at 8:00. I was off on Thursdays and spent my morning sidewalk counseling at a local inner-city women's clinic that performed abortions. In the afternoon I worked at the soup kitchen located in the hall of my church.

On Fridays, I spent the day in prayer in a small chapel inside St. Charles. Spending time in prayer was essential while in this ministry. It is when God would minister to me and refresh me. He would fill me up so I was able to continue to give to those whom I was ministering to. I also fasted every Friday on bread and water as a means of strengthening myself spiritually.

I went to the clinic every Thursday which was one of the days that abortions were scheduled. I went with the goal of seeing women turn back from carrying through with their plans. I would stand and pray on the sidewalk in front of the clinic. I also passed out educational brochures and tracts to whomever would take them. In addition, I spoke through the window which led to the waiting room on the inside of the clinic. I would say that there were places that support women with "problem pregnancies." I told them about The Little Flower Home.

One day a young girl was being escorted by two adults into the clinic. I could see that the girl was crying. I guessed that she didn't want to have her baby's life terminated. I spoke through the window as usual. A little later, the woman came out and asked questions about the options that I spoke of. She also took our brochures. A short time later, the young girl came out and we spoke with her as well. She went back into the clinic, only to immediately come out with the two adults that accompanied her inside. Within the week, the young girl named Jamie called the home. She visited the home and decided that she would stay at the home until her baby was born. She had never wanted to have her baby aborted. She was being coerced by her father and step-mother.

Once Jamie came to the home, she told me that as she sat in the waiting area of the clinic, she could hear me singing a song. It is a song that I wrote while in prayer, that I frequently sang outside the windows of the one level building. It is sung to the melody of "Rock-a-Bye Baby." She heard me sing these words, *"My heart is beating. I can feel pain. I have ten toes and fingers like you. We are the same, both thirsting for love. O please let me love you, Mommy."* As I think on the words of this song today, I wonder if the neglected child within me related to the unborn babies whose feelings were being disregarded. It was as if I became the voice for the voiceless babies.

In my one year in this ministry, most of the residents came to the home because their parents told them that they had to either choose to abort their baby or leave their home. Within months, the majority of girls who came to the home because of that ultimatum, were welcomed back home after their parents realized that they had a precious, innocent grandchild who was soon to be born. Barbara was an example of this, but only with her second pregnancy. When she came to the home she had already had an abortion that her mother forced upon her. She took Barbara to the local women's hospital, paid two thousand dollars and presto! Barbara's baby was "terminated." The staff at the hospital is directed to use that nice, neat term instead of the actual term that it is. The truth is that her baby's life was innocently snuffed out—killed.

Barbara's family was wealthy and they didn't want their family to live with the shame of Barbara's misdeed. But when Barbara got pregnant a second time, she put her foot down. She suffered the consequences though. Her mother also put her foot down. She told Barbara that if she didn't have an abortion, she would have to leave their home. Thankfully, Barbara chose to let her baby live, and then discovered the home. In the end, her mother relented when she met her beautiful grandson named Seth and invited them both to live with her.

My most memorable and extraordinary experience involves Leslie. When she came to the home, she had previously been doing hard drugs while spending most of her time living on the street. She was seventeen and had already had two abortions. She decided she wanted to keep her third baby. She even stopped doing drugs. Leslie was three months pregnant when one day she complained of cramping and spotting. I took her to the hospital to have her examined, but unfortunately they couldn't do much. They sent her home and told her to have bed rest. That evening, the girls and I huddled around her in her bedroom. Leslie was in pain and very afraid of losing her baby. We prayed with her that night in an effort to encourage and console her.

In the early morning hours she woke me. She was frantic. "I'm bleeding—a lot! And it hurts so much! Take me to the hospital!" As we ventured to leave, Leslie ran to the bathroom, and I followed. She sat down on the toilet just when the baby fell from her. The baby slipped off to the outside of the bowl and landed on the rug. I picked him up and held him in my hands. He was a boy. He was about three inches long and flesh colored. He had his two arms, two legs, and webbed fingers and toes. Leslie named her baby Steven Mark and then we dedicated him to God.

Not knowing what to do with the baby, I placed him in a bowl in the refrigerator. I then took Leslie to the hospital. While Leslie was being examined, the hospital staff asked us for the baby. Well—they actually asked for the "fetus." However, Leslie had seen with her own eyes that she had birthed a baby and this made all the difference in the world. Leslie refused to hand over her baby to the hospital to examine unless they promised to return it to her. She was adamant upon burying her baby. The usual procedure was to dispose of the premature bodies in the incinerator. The hospital staff agreed to return Leslie's baby, so I went home to retrieve his body.

Many weeks later, after my unrelenting phone calls, the hospital finally agreed to release Leslie's premature baby to us. Millie and I got busy planning a burial service. A local pastor offered a small plot in the church cemetery, as well as a service at graveside, and a friend of the home built a precious, small white casket. The service was simple but profound; a beautiful testament to the fact that life is a gift, one that should be honored and graciously welcomed.

Triscah is another girl who stands out in my mind. Triscah came to the home at the age of nineteen. She was from Kenya and had recently immigrated to the US to live with her aunt's family. Her goal while living in the States was to receive a college degree in nursing. Shortly after she arrived however, she found herself to be pregnant with her uncle's baby. He had raped her while back at home in Kenya. "It is a common practice," Triscah told me. "*However common it is, it is still mortifying,*" I thought.

Triscah stands out amongst all the other girls because she shone with the knowledge and love of God. She and I prayed together frequently. Her faith was inspiring to me. She was different from the other girls because while most of them were depressed, negative, and often filled with self-pity, she had a joy about her and a peace that stemmed from the grace of God.

Triscah felt that to abort her baby would mean to kill it, so she made the decision to bring her baby to term and then offer it up for adoption. Once Triscah delivered her baby girl, she was adopted by a loving Christian family of whom I got to meet. Triscah then went back to living with her aunt and returned to college to finish her studies. Triscah is a hero in my eyes.

Christmas at the home was nearing. I had a friend who committed a year to rescuing the unborn, as a member of a national organization, Operation Rescue. He traveled with this organization while visiting clinics that were known for performing the highest number of abortions in the country. Jordan would join others in creating and implementing plans that would keep clinics from performing abortions. All this was done in a prayerful and peaceful way. Jordan spent months in jail for blocking doors of clinics, and others had spent years in jail.

This Christmas Jordan had come home. He and his father had created a plan that would keep a local abortion clinic from performing abortions on Christmas Eve. They built two locks meant to hold five people each. Each one would be placed at an entrance to the clinic.

Millie, the other house manager, was planning on participating in the rescue, but I was not. I spent the week leading up to Christmas Eve in bed with the flu. However, on the day before the rescue, I felt God calling me to join the rescue, and coincidentally, I had noticed I was feeling better. Jordan told me there was room for one more person. I was the final and tenth person to join the rescue. Also included were two men in their seventies, two women in their fifties, and a fifteen year old girl. I was twenty-six years old at the time.

The morning of the rescue we met at our church, St. Charles. Fr. Randall met us there, gave us some guidance, and said a prayer of blessing over us. At the clinic, we had a large group of Christian supporters present who watched out for us, encouraged us, and prayed for us. It was truly an anointed experience. As the police approached us, we prayed. They attempted to free us from the locks, but were unable. Our arms were locked from inside large metal tubes. The only way to be freed of these locks was for us to voluntarily unlock ourselves. We told the officers that we would unlock ourselves at the appointed hour when abortions were no longer scheduled.

Because of our supporters and the local TV stations that observed us, it was a peaceful and calm event. We participators and supporters simply prayed aloud and sang our praises to God. I was surprised at how much peace I felt. It was as if I was surrounded by a bubble; removed from chaos, and negativity.

We unlocked ourselves at the appointed hour. We were carefully placed in the police vans, as we were under the eye of the TV cameras, and then brought to the city-police holding cells. Bonnie's husband witnessed me on his TV screen being carried by two officers, one at my feet and the other at my hands, and placed in the van. I was mortified because Bonnie knew nothing of my deep involvement in the pro-life movement. She was pro-choice, as I had been before God convicted me of the truth of the matter.

Once we arrived at the city prison, the ladies were placed together, as were the men. We spent the time praying and praising God in song. We were free of anxiety and remained in peace.

After two hours, we were released without arraignment! The judge decided to let us go without even a hearing because it was Christmas Eve. We were never even fingerprinted or mugged, so we left there without a blemish on our record. As we approached the exits, we found our faithful supporters. They had followed the vans to the police department to make sure that we were well treated and that our rights were protected. They also prayed for our safety and quick release. Once their prayers were answered, they offered us rides back to our cars which were at the clinic, and from there we each drove home to prepare to welcome the Christ Child on Christmas day.

As I lay down to sleep that evening, I could only hope that the women who were planning on terminating the life of their unborn babies that Christmas Eve, took it as a sign that they were meant to welcome the gift of the child within their wombs. My prayer was that they found the hope that is offered to them in the form of the little Christ Child, our Savior Jesus Christ.

Since my year at The Little Flower Home, a relationship with Maria was rekindled. Maria was nineteen when she had her baby, but mentally she was about thirteen. She wasn't capable of caring for her child, so her father and step-mother adopted her son. Because of her mental disability, she received Social Security Insurance and housing. Maria and I didn't form a special relationship while she was at the home. It came a year or so later.

One day, as she sat in her apartment watching the six o'clock evening news, she saw a segment which focused on St. Charles Church. It caused her to remember that I attended that church every Sunday and the weekly prayer meetings which were held on Thursdays. She thought, *"It's Thursday. If I get a ride to the church by 7:30, maybe I'll see Holly."*

I was right where she thought I was.

As I sat waiting for the prayer meeting to begin, in walked Maria. She walked right up to me and embraced me. "Oh my gosh, it's Maria from The Home!" I exclaimed. She proceeded to tell me how she came to be there at that moment. I was quite surprised, especially because I didn't have knowledge that I meant anything to her while she was at the home. At this later date, I found Maria to be hungry for the Lord as she proceeded to attend church and weekly prayer meetings regularly. This was unlike her when she was living at the home. Gradually, I found myself in a mentoring relationship with Maria. I became her friend who was there for her emotionally, spiritually, and physically.

Chapter Five

They had just revived my sister and now she is lying here fighting for her life and the life of her unborn baby. My friends and I lay our hands on Elizabeth and pray for a miracle. "Oh God, you say in Your Word, 'Where two or three are gathered in My name, there I will be in their midst'... 'Whatever you ask of My father in My name, I will do.'" (Matthew 18:19,20 & John 15:16). And He did!

Nicky was not the only person in my life whom I comforted in his last days. It seems quite unusual that there have been a good number of them. Even more unusual is how several of these people were family members who happened to return to live in Rhode Island, only to spend their last days before passing. I tend to think that these occurrences were not coincidences, but God incidences. I think that God used me to pray or intercede for them.

It is important to note that just about all of my relatives from either side of my family moved out of state—most moved to Florida. I mention this because when a family member moved back to Rhode Island, I happened to be the only relative in the state and available to come to their aid. There was only one person who didn't die and that was my sister Elizabeth.

My sister has always moved back and forth from Rhode Island to Florida over the years. She just happened to live minutes away from me when I got a call from my mother from Florida that Elizabeth was in a critical state at Rhode Island Hospital.

When I made it to the hospital, I found that Elizabeth was just hanging onto her life by a thread. Her heart had stopped while being transported to the hospital and the medics had revived her. Her body was in a septic shock, which means that her blood stream and tissues were infected. She had three major things going wrong with her body, including pneumonia and kidney failure. She was not only fighting for her life, but that of her unborn baby.

During this scary time, I was at my sister's bedside daily. We had never been close prior to this moment, but that didn't matter. I turned to God in earnest to pray that He would spare her life and that of my unborn niece or nephew. I put them on the prayer list at my church, and had many of my friends praying up a storm.

One day my friends decided to come to the hospital and pray for my sister. My pastor Fr. Randall accompanied my friends as well. We met in a conference room down the hall from my sister's room and had a prayer meeting. We then got to go into my sister's room where she lay in an induced coma. We laid our hands on her and prayed for healing. This is what I did every day when I visited her bedside. I also sang her songs like "Be Not Afraid." I remember singing those words so vividly. It was as if the words were written just for us at that very moment.

On one of the occasions that I visited my sister, an extraordinary thing happened. After weeks of visiting Elizabeth, I arrived at my sister's room only to find her bed empty. That fact made my heart skip a few beats. I inquired of her whereabouts and was relieved to hear that she was moved out of the intensive care unit because her health had improved.

I will never forget the way my sister appeared when I found her. I walked into a room with four beds occupied with patients. I looked past every single one and concluded that Elizabeth was not there. I then did a double take and discovered that I had been mistaken. Elizabeth *was* in that room. I didn't recognize her face because she looked so different, as compared to the time in intensive care, as well as the time before her illness. Elizabeth has always suffered from severe depression to the point of wanting to kill herself. Therefore, she was not a happy or optimistic person, and rarely sported a smile. As I gazed upon her face, it was as if a light was on inside her head. Her face had a bright, happy glow.

As I pondered that transformation for days afterward, I decided it had to be all of the prayers said for her. God worked a miracle inside of my sister's heart. My sister to this day speaks of that time when she was ill. The memories of that period in her life bring warm feelings. It was a time when she had many people caring for her. It made her feel special and loved, which she had rarely felt. She will also never forget the prayers of my friends. Even though she was in a coma-state, she had the knowledge that my friends, mere strangers to her, were there and had cared about her. It touched her heart.

Another awesome miracle was that of my nephew Billy. While Elizabeth was still critical and in a coma-state, an OB-GYN resident approached my mother and me to suggest that we might want to terminate Elizabeth's unborn baby. Amongst several potent medications, Elizabeth was being administered a very serious one called Vancomycin. Doctors very rarely administer this drug because of the harsh and extensive side effects. They warned us that the baby could be born with critical health defects. Mom and I responded that we would not terminate the baby. The OB-GYN resident thought we were making a mistake.

As we prayed for my sister's health during this critical period, we also prayed for her unborn baby. I asked God to protect her baby from ill health, and to allow it to be born at full term. On February 25th 1993, Billy was born right on time! Elizabeth had a healthy, smooth delivery.

Billy appeared to be healthy in all aspects. The state sent a home health service to Elizabeth's home to evaluate Billy's physical and mental health regularly for two years and they never found a single problem.

Billy was a healthy, beautiful baby boy. A miracle baby for sure! God felt it in His heart to allow Elizabeth the opportunity to meet her son and to care for him until the appointed time when God would call him to Himself. What a blessing and a privilege.

Again I found myself at the bed of an ailing relative. My mother's aunt whom we called Taunt ("aunt" in French) was a "snow bird." She was born in Rhode Island but later in life bought a house in Florida to spend the winter seasons. She was a devout Baptist. Although her long-time partner of thirty years was a woman, she attended church every Sunday and read her Bible regularly. I loved Taunt. In my young adult years we became close. She was always there for me and supported me in many ways.

Every now and then Taunt helped me out financially. She was a very successful woman, and to her credit, she was generous with her wealth. She never forgot her humble beginnings. I especially remember Taunt's generosity during my teaching years. For two consecutive years, Taunt donated money so that I could purchase literature books for my fifth grade class. I'm sure she would've continued to do so in the following years, but a heart attack claimed her life at the early age of seventy-two.

Taunt had a serious case of diabetes, type two. Due to this disease she had a poor heart and was going blind. Taunt had many close calls those last years. She suffered a heart attack, and several congestive heart failures before the second heart attack claimed her life.

Every time Taunt was hospitalized she happened to be in Rhode Island, and I just happened to be the only relative in town.

I spent many days at Taunt's bedside praying for her. We prayed together as well. She loved it when I prayed for her, especially at those times when she was unable to do so. Taunt believed in my prayers. I never judged Taunt because of her homosexual lifestyle. I left that to God. I just loved her and prayed that He would welcome her in His loving arms on the day that she would pass from this world. I asked Him to have mercy on her, and to look not on her sins, but on the blood of the Lamb that was shed for her.

I remember the last time I saw Taunt. She had just been approved to check out from the hospital. She was immediately returning to Florida, as the winter season was well on its way. I received a phone call in about a week that she suffered from a fatal heart attack. She took her last breath in her Florida home, never to make it to another hospital bed.

The next bed I was to sit by would be my grandfather whom we called Granddad. Granddad was my mother's father. It is interesting to note that I was not close to my grandfather, nor my mother's mother. They were divorced when my mother was a child. As I was growing up, we didn't see a lot of my grandparents. Both grandparents were dysfunctional with their own dysfunctional stories of childhood.

My grandfather remarried and became involved in his wife's family. He was also an alcoholic. My grandmother married seven times. She was a promiscuous woman, and known to cheat on her husbands. She also had times of being emotionally unstable. My grandparents were disconnected from their daughter and grandchildren. Hence, when I came to the assistance of Granddad and later Grammy, it wasn't out of love for them, but for God and the desire to please Him. I also think that God gave me the desire to want to be there for them, and as time went on, I grew to love them.

Granddad was in need of support after his wife Betty passed away because she had cared for him and his needs. At this time my husband and I began visiting him regularly at his home and often took him out for a bite to eat. Several years later, Granddad was diagnosed with colon cancer. Following surgery to remove the cancer, his health quickly declined. Granddad had also suffered a stroke several years prior which left him unable to use his left side. With this combination of health problems, he became unable to care for himself and his home. Because Mom lived in Florida, I volunteered to help find a nursing home that would provide a safe place for him to reside.

With much research and several visits to local nursing homes, I chose the home where Granddad would live. I visited Granddad frequently, and it was only in his last days when dementia began to settle in, that I was able to pray for him in his presence. Unfortunately, when in his right mind, Granddad wasn't open to hear about God. He had a rebellious attitude towards God. When it was evident that his time was near to pass from this world, I brought Fr. Hugh with me to pray for Granddad. Together we asked God to forgive him of his sins; to look upon Granddad with mercy, and to receive his soul into His arms of rest and peace.

Gram, my mother's mother, also had a rebellious spirit toward God. She behaved as if she hated God. This was how I found Gram to be when I first began to visit her in an assisted living residence. Oddly enough, Gram, who lived for fifteen years in an in-law apartment with my mother in Florida, and had planned to spend her last days there, ended up back in Rhode Island. When Gram was still living with Mom, dementia started to settle in. Gram was doing lots of unstable things which often led her into the arms of the police. In fear of being put into a mental institution, Gram hopped on a plane to move back to Rhode Island.

It was in no time at all, however, that Gram ended up in the care of the local police once again. We got a phone call letting us know that she was admitted in the ward for the mentally challenged. They had her pretty drugged up when we finally had her released. Once released, Gram found herself an assisted living residence an hour away from my home. It was then that I began visiting Gram, whom I hardly knew, on a regular basis.

I didn't look forward to my visits with Gram. Even so, I visited her in Westerly once a month for several years. It was difficult to take the time to go because I had two small children at home. I tried taking them with me but that didn't work out well because of the energy that two little boys generate. Just the drive alone took two hours from my day. Once I arrived, I didn't feel welcomed or appreciated. By this time Gram was really losing her mind. She told many stories which stemmed from paranoia, thus they weren't usually pleasant stories. Gram was not a happy person, so I found her moods quite difficult to bear.

Every time I visited Gram, I brought her two things that she loved, a bouquet of flowers and a Dunkin Donuts coffee. I had to be careful not to put my coffee down within her reach because if I did, I would find it gone. Gram would have drunk it! She could down a cup of coffee like it was water. I also massaged her legs and feet because Gram was an over-sized woman with poor circulation. I tried to make Gram feel special. Every now and then I'd slip in something about God.

I would try to get Gram to think about what would happen once she left this world. She hated the thought. She had never even had a will written, making it difficult on my mother and uncle when she did pass. I think she was afraid that there was a hell and she might end up there. Or maybe it was because she wanted no part of God because she blamed Him for the unfortunate things that happened in her life.

Mom told me of an incident that might've contributed to Gram's feelings towards God. As a child, Gram lived a very comfortable lifestyle. Her family enjoyed many luxuries such as a full time housekeeper. However, Gram's life fell apart in 1929, on Black Monday, when the stock market crashed. Her family lost everything.

Gram's family, who had resided in Maine, was forced to move to Rhode Island to live with her aunt, on her mother's side. Her uncle didn't want them there so he treated them very poorly. Gram came to despise her uncle who was often very cruel to her. I never did hear details of Gram's life from her, nor did she share her thoughts and feelings with me, thus I can't say for sure why she got angry at the mention of God.

After driving to Westerly for two years, a blessing in disguise occurred. I received a call from my mother that Gram was rushed to the hospital. She went into congestive heart failure and they didn't think she was going to make it. When I visited her in the hospital I prayed to God that He would take her, but that if he didn't, He would have a good reason. Gram pulled through all on her own. I figured God wanted me to pray some more for Gram's soul so that when her time did come, she would go straight into His arms.

The blessing in this incident came in the form that Mom let me move Gram to a home that was closer to mine. I wanted to be able to visit her weekly and to be there readily if she needed me. I also wanted her removed from the assisted living because of what we found out when she was hospitalized. The doctors told us that her arm was broken. When questioned, the staff from the assisted living residence said that she had fallen and they didn't think she had hurt herself. I was livid.

I had always felt that this home wasn't providing quality service and care, but Gram was familiar with it and didn't want to experience change, as is common with Alzheimer's patients. This was her latest diagnosis. Clearly, Gram needed more care, so I began my search for a nursing home that was close to my home.

I was happy to find a very nice home only five minutes away. My elderly aunt on my father's side was living there, so I had the testimony of relatives that it was a good choice. On the day that Gram was being transported to Hopkins Manor, I hurried over to be there when she arrived. I knew she would be very upset to be arriving at a place that was unfamiliar to her, only to be welcomed by perfect strangers.

However, as I first gazed at Gram's face and disposition, it was like I was looking at another person. She was calm and appeared happy. She didn't have an ounce of trepidation. The medics told me that she didn't give them any opposition or complaints as they handled her. This did not sound like Gram! In the past, medics had to use a restraint on her.

This day was a pivotal one in my mind. From this day forward, Gram was like a different person, one whom I was happy to be around. She smiled throughout the day and seemed careless and free. She never complained or spoke negatively about the staff or other residents, as she had been known to do. Everybody there spoke so cheerfully of Gram. I can't tell you how or why this change occurred. Nurses told me that sometimes when an Alzheimer's patient suffers a trauma, or near-death experience, his or her personality changes. Whatever the reason, I felt blessed by God. It became a pleasure to visit Gram.

Gram came to love me even though she could not tell you my name. I knew this because of the way that she responded to me when I walked into the room. Gram not only had a loss of her mind, but she also rarely spoke at this stage of the Alzheimer's. She could not tell you I was her granddaughter, but she knew I was someone who loved her, and whom she loved in return. One time I brought her a rose. When it was time for me to leave, she gave the rose back to me (most likely she forgot that I gave it to her). This was a big deal to me because Gram was never a giving person in the past. Here she was, a woman with so little, and she gave my gift back to me as a gift from herself. This brought tears to my eyes at the time.

I frequently brought Gram stuffed animals, particularly bright and interactive ones. She loved to hold them as if they were babies. In those last days, it was as if she was the child and I, the adult.

Even though Gram didn't talk, I still did. I would talk to her, pray with her, read and sing to her. Although I had to practically yell in her ear for her to hear me. At this time, I could talk all I wanted about God and receive no opposition. I made friends with the residents there and often we'd all gather outdoors and pray together. There were a few under the age of fifty and had serious disabilities. I felt much empathy for them. I enjoyed speaking with them as I tried to spread some sunshine in their lives. Knowing them definitely made me feel grateful for my own life.

As the end was near, Gram was admitted in the hospital for pneumonia. I remember sitting beside Gram's hospital bed praying for her. As I prayed, I had a vision. I saw Jesus clothed in a radiant light wearing a white robe. He had His arms open and said, "*Come to me.*" I felt that God was calling Gram, and the good news was that He was beckoning her with open arms. He was welcoming her into heaven.

Gram eventually was discharged from the hospital but it wasn't before long that Gram passed. I had peace with the knowledge that she was with God. My Nana made a comment about my grandmother passing. She said something like, "I hope you're praying for your grandmother. She lived a very immoral life." I could tell she feared that Gram was not with God. I told her, "Gram is in heaven. I know it." I could tell she didn't believe it. I feel however, that God accepted my prayers and sacrifices for Gram and this is what helped to save her soul. Similarly, Abraham begged God to save Sodom and Gomorrah—that He would have mercy on the sinners there for the sake of the righteous (Genesis 18:23-32).

Not much time passed before Nana's life also came to an end. My Nana was also an intercessor. She interceded for every member of her family including her four children, ten grandchildren, and twelve great-grandchildren. Twice over the years I fell away from God, but Nana prayed me right back. I knew it was her prayers that God answered.

All through my adult years, whenever I visited Nana, we stopped to pray together. I treasured those moments. For twenty years, prior to Nana's passing, we had interceded for our family, that they would come to know Christ and receive salvation.

In Nana's final years she was nursed in her home by my aunt. Eventually however, Nana was moved to a nearby nursing home. I visited Nana frequently in the short time before she passed. Each time I visited, I prayed out loud for her and for all of our family, just the way she would if she could. Nana had a stroke in her last days and wasn't able to speak. We didn't know if Nana was consciously aware of her surroundings because she had a blank stare most of the time.

On one occasion, as I started to sing "How Great Thou Art" she went from a blank stare to crying. Her tears subsided as I continued to sing, but then it happened again when I began to sing "Amazing Grace." Within the first few words of these songs, Nana started to cry. Those two moments were the only moments of recognition that I saw on Nana's face in those last days.

God finally took her, and it was an answer to my prayers, because she was visibly in pain those last days. Nana died at the age of ninety six. I can't wait for the day when I meet Nana again in heaven, and join together with the other family members that we helped to pray into heaven. And once there, I will also be happy to greet Nicky, Taunt, Granddad and Gram!

What a glorious day it will be!

Chapter Six

I lie in bed sobbing and cry out to God, "Why can't you give me a man to love and who will love me in return?!" In the silence of my empty apartment, I can almost hear my heart breaking. I know that I will never see Nathan again after tonight's fight. I didn't hear a reply from God, but I did get one within a few days.

Unfortunately, I continued to seek love from men. After my conversion, I decided to give up sexual activity with men, but I failed in this attempt. I began dating a wonderful Christian man and we were falling in love. We refrained from sexual intercourse for quite some time, but eventually we gave in to our desires. It seemed like in no time at all, things started to go wrong in our relationship. One evening we had a big fight which led to the end of our relationship. That evening as I lay in bed, I sobbed and cried out to God. I was in so much pain. This man I dated was one of the nicest men I had ever gone out with.

Following that mournful night, for two nights in a row, I woke up at the same time, 3:16 a.m. On the third day, I was with a mature Christian friend and told him what had happened. He told me that sometimes God wakes us up to talk to us because it is then that we are still and quiet, and more apt to hear Him. He told me that if it happened again to ask God what it was that He wanted to say to me.

A similar thing happened in the book of Samuel from the Old Testament. As Samuel, who was just a boy, lay asleep, he heard the Lord call him.

> "A third time the LORD called, 'Samuel!' And Samuel got up and went to Eli and said, 'Here I am; you called me.' Then Eli realized that the Lord was calling the boy. So Eli told Samuel, 'Go and lie down, and if he calls you, say, 'Speak, Lord, for your servant is listening'" (1 Samuel 3:8,9).

That same evening, as I lay sleeping, it happened a third time. I woke up at 3:16. I took my friend's advice and just listened. It was hard because my thoughts kept wondering away from God to the details of my daily life. But then something came to my mind. I was brought back to the moment when the angel in Medjugorje spoke those special words to me. It was as if God was reiterating to me those words. *"Holly, I told you that I love you. I think you are beautiful. Why are you searching elsewhere?"* That evening changed me. It was as if the words stuck this time; as if I believed them.

Following that evening, I stopped altogether looking for a man—my possible husband to be. I stopped walking into a crowded room and seeking the attention of a man. As a matter of fact, I had a new philosophy. I told my Christian girl friends of my new philosophy. "When God feels it is time for me to meet the man that He has for me, he will just appear. I don't need to look for him. I don't even have to leave my house to find a man. God will just send him knocking on my door." Two years later, these words came to pass. My husband came knocking on my door.

Another change that occurred in me is that I vowed to wait to have sexual intercourse until my wedding day. Some people might say that I became a "born-again virgin." God gave me the grace to keep this vow. I abstained from sex for seven years until my wedding day at the age of thirty.

I now went to God to fill me up with His love and not to men. The truth is that no mortal man can ever satisfy the deep longings that we all bear within our souls. Only Jesus can give us the water to drink that will quench our thirst once and for all. This is what Jesus offered the Samaritan woman in John 4. She sought love and fulfillment from her five ex-husbands and in her current live-in partner. Jesus knew this about her and cared enough for her to want to give her what she needed—what she so desired. Jesus tells her in John 4:14, "Whoever drinks of the water that I will give him shall never thirst; but the water that I will give him will become in him a well of water springing up to eternal life."

One day I heard a song from my roommate's CD. It is called "You Light up My Life" by Carole King, not to be mistaken for the song by Debbie Boone. As I listened to the words of the song, I realized that they described the exact way that I felt about God. Some of the words go like this:

"You light up my life, like a sunrise in the morning. You make me believe anything is possible. I didn't have a dream to my name. Darkness was mine, it was such a shame. I never knew how rich I could be. Loving you has left me with nothing to contain. You really light up my life. You give me faith, and hope, and love, and light."

This was my love song to God. Regarding this song, I made a pact with God. I told God that if He made it possible for me to love a man enough to marry him, then I would sing this song at my wedding and dedicate it to Him. Two years later on my wedding day, I came through with my promise. I told my family and friends who were gathered at the wedding reception that I loved Dan, but it wouldn't have been possible for me to love him without God's love that flowed through me.

However, before that day was to happen, God needed to do some things in my heart to prepare me for this kind of love. My heart was still broken from childhood and unable to give love the way God intends in marriage. He needed to heal my heart.

That healing process began while I was at a St. Charles prayer meeting. Fr. Randall had invited the members to come up and kiss the eight foot cross in the front of the room. He frequently gave the message that to follow Jesus; one must pick up his cross and carry it, just as Jesus did. That evening, I never made it to the eight foot cross. It was as if the cross came to me.

Father had been sharing "words of knowledge" as we worshiped God in song. He spoke a word that said, "God wants to heal someone of abuse." Within a few minutes, I began sobbing my eyes out. I gradually became weaker as pain overflowed from the depths of my soul. I was brought to my knees, and as I became weaker, I ended up on the floor in the fetal position. I finally became flat out prostrate on my face, as I sobbed and pounded the floor with my fists. My face was lying in a puddle of my tears. This lasted close to an hour. I had no pictures in my mind. No memories. I had no idea why I was crying.

Eventually I became still and quiet while lying on the floor. Then I heard it again—Father's words. He repeated the same words as before. And it began again. The sobbing. The pain—from the depths of my being. I knew from the way that I was responding to those words, that the word of knowledge was for me.

By the end of the prayer meeting, my body felt as if I had surgery. I couldn't even stand on my own. My friend helped me up and gave me a chair, and then she called Father over to speak with me. I told him that God revealed to me that I had been abused, but that I didn't have any memories. I started thinking of the people that it could've been. I thought of my brother. "*Yes,*" I thought. "*He did sexually abuse me.*" Prior to this moment, I had never acknowledged it. I never said, "My brother abused me." But I knew there was someone else who caused me deeper pain—the deepest pain. I thought, "*My father?*"

"Yes. My father."

I remember what I did the following day. I drove to the church with my friend who was with me the previous night, to pray about what happened then. I remember that she read a verse from the Bible; the words that Jesus spoke while hanging on the cross. She read, "Father, forgive them. For they know not what they do," as found in Luke 23:24. Forgiveness would be a recurring message that God was to give me over the following ten years of my life—until the time when I would completely let go of the bitterness, resentment and hatred in my heart towards my father. I was willing from the start to forgive because I knew it was the will of God, but truly living it out was another matter altogether.

I spent a year in the trenches of the healing process, but God spent the previous years preparing me for the battle. It was after I had come out of the trenches to a place of wellness and wholeness that I could look back in retrospect and see how God worked in my life to prepare me for the moment when He would reveal the ugly truth.

God's first means of preparation came in the form of filling me up with the knowledge of how much He loved me. This brought me to trust Him. He also brought me to an intimate union with the suffering of Jesus Christ. This was important because when the time did come when I was to endure much pain and suffering, I was able to unite myself with Jesus and found solace in the fact that I wasn't alone in my pain. He did this during the time that I spent on my second trip to Medjugorje, and then a year and a half later on a pilgrimage to Fatima, Portugal. On both trips I had experiences that brought me face to face with the sufferings of Jesus.

During the time of preparation, God started to bring things to the surface. One evening I woke up in the middle of the night and was completely drenched from head to toe as if I had just gotten out of the shower. This had never happened to me before and I didn't have a clue as to why. I later surmised that I must have had a terrible nightmare, as I soon began to have them frequently.

Shortly after that evening, I had a nightmare that involved several men chasing me with guns and they were trying to kill me. Prior to this time, I always had a recurring nightmare which started at a very young age. It had to do with a dog, or several dogs attacking me viciously.

These dreams always ended with a dog that had its teeth in my hand, and I couldn't get it loose. Then my dream would end. The pain is what impacted me the most. Fear—then pain. I have never been attacked by a dog, nor have I witnessed such a thing. However, later while on my journey of healing, I would discover that dogs took the place of the men who hurt me.

At this point in time I started to have recurring nightmares that were now about men who were trying to catch me to either rape me, or kill me. Sometimes I did get caught and then I'd wake up and cry out to Jesus. Sometimes there was just one man and sometimes it was a gang of men. The dreams may have been slightly different but the feelings that they evoked were always the same—**fear** and **pain**.

Soon after the nightmares began, I took the job at The Little Flower Home. During my time there, I heard countless stories from the girls about their experiences with sexual abuse. Some cases were about date rape and others were of incest. The majority of the girls had a story such as one of these. It was of no wonder that the girls led a promiscuous lifestyle and at such a young age. I feel that hearing these stories subconsciously brought my own experiences to the surface. It was while I was living at the home that God brought about the revelation that I too was a victim of incest.

There were other things that God used to prepare me. Every now and then a person would come up to me and tell me out of the blue, "You are going to suffer." There was a particular lady from my church who told me this. She was one of those ladies that you always saw praying in the church. At least twice she came up to me, looked deep into my eyes and told me those chilling words. I couldn't understand how it would be true because I was so happy and in love with the Lord at the time. I was filled with the joy that one possesses when on their honeymoon.

On one occasion, this same lady came up to me and gave me a stunning picture as a gift. Mind you, I didn't really know this lady. It was a framed sketch that she had created of the crucified head of Christ, which bared the crown of thorns and a horrifying look of torment on the face of Jesus. When I gazed at the picture, I was immediately brought to think of the vision that I had in the stone when I was in Medjugorje. I was amazed!

It is true that I did not welcome the thought of suffering, but because God gave me the knowledge of what was to come, it assured me that He was in control. It helped me to trust in Him. Similarly, Jesus prepared the disciples for what was to come during the time prior to His suffering and death. He said to them in John 16:1, "I have told you this so that you may not fall away."

A few times I gathered with girlfriends to pray for one another. We would seek God's intentions for each other and pray for one another's needs. Concerning me, we felt that God was saying that I was going to suffer. On one occasion, my friend asked God to give me a promise that I could hold on to; a hope that I could cling to. As we prayed, God lead us to the scripture found in Leviticus 20:24. "But to you I have said, 'Their land shall be your possession, a land flowing with milk and honey. I am giving it to you as your own; I the Lord God have set you apart from the other nations." Very interesting to note however, are the verses that come immediately prior to this verse. These verses came to my attention once I was in the midst of my suffering. The verses listed prior to verse 24 describe various acts of incest that God was not pleased with. He states in verse 23, "Do not conform therefore, to the customs of the nations whom I am driving out of your way, because all of these things that they have done have filled me with disgust for them."

Another promise that I clung to while carrying my cross is found in Joel 2:25 "I will repay you for the years the locusts have eaten." I read this scripture and believed that there would be a day when all that had been stolen from me by the evil one, God would restore to me. This truth filled me with hope.

I believe I was visited by another angel on the eve of the New Year. Fr. Randall was holding an all night vigil in the church where we prayed in the coming year of 1992. I was sitting next to my friend Derik. At one point in the evening I felt a tap on my shoulder. I looked to him and said, "What?"

He replied, "What? What do you want?"

"You tapped me on my shoulder," I retorted. "No I didn't, but *you* tapped me on *my* shoulder."

"No, I did not," was his final reply. "Then who did?"

Later that night we discussed what had happened, but we couldn't figure it out. I felt that it was an angel. We were both single at the time and I knew Derik liked me, so I secretly thought that maybe he was the one for me and this was a sign. I eventually discovered that my hunch was incorrect.

Within a few months of that New Year, the revelation of the incest came. After a few more months, I bumped into Derik in the chapel of the church. I hadn't seen him since New Year's Eve because he ended up going to a seminary in Canada to discern a vocation in the priesthood. When we saw each other, we spent time catching up. I ended up sharing with him what God was doing in my life regarding my inner healing. He too had a story to tell and it was incredibly a lot like my own.

Derik shared with me that he was molested by a female babysitter when he was young. He shared that while at the seminary, God brought up his past to bring healing to his heart. He shared details that sounded so familiar to mine in the way that God was dealing with him. It was incredible to share with one another, as we were able to relate to one another, and thus find understanding and strength in the knowledge that we were not alone.

Later that day, I had an "Ah ha!" moment. I came to believe the meaning of why we both were tapped on the shoulder, by which I believe, was an angel. For the New Year, God had the plan of healing the broken, wounded hearts of two of His beloved children. Derik, like me, also welcomed the will of God, because He also had felt assured of the Father's love for Him.

Another major tool God used as preparation is a well-known book called "Hinds' Feet on High Places" by Hannah Hurnard[2]. I must tell you about this book because the story therein is something that God used in my life over many years. God speaks to us in many different ways and a book is just one of them. Following the conclusion of the book, God brought the revelation, and from thence I would find myself remembering parts that I read from it, which comforted me, strengthened me, and guided me.

The book is an allegory about two main characters, the Shepherd, who is Jesus, and Much-Afraid, who represents a child of God (you and me). Much-Afraid has things about herself that she would like the Shepherd to change. She possesses a crooked mouth, malformed feet and intense fear that has kept her from doing many things, hence, the title of her name. She heard that the Shepherd brings people to the High Places, which were the very tops of the mountains surrounding her village, and there

---

[2] Hannah Hurnard, *Hinds' Feet on High Places* (Tyndale House Publishers)

He would change them and make them into all that they desired.

But before the Shepherd could take her to the High Places, He needed Much Afraid to agree to let Him turn her feet into hinds' feet, for that was the only way she could travel on the treacherous mountain terrain. She also needed to have her name changed, because she couldn't enter the Kingdom of Love with a name from the Fearing family.

The Shepherd also told her, "No one is allowed to enter the Kingdom of Love unless they have the flower of Love already blooming in their hearts." Then He asked her, "Has Love been planted in your heart Much-Afraid?"

"I think that what is growing there is a great longing to experience the joy of natural, human love and to learn to love supremely one person who will love me in return." She added, "I don't think I see the kind of Love that you are talking about, at least nothing like the Love which I see in you.'"

"Then will you let Me plant the seed of true Love there now?"

"Much-Afraid shrank back. She said, "'I have been told that if you really love someone, you give that loved one the power to hurt and pain you in a way nothing else can.'"

"But it is so happy to love. Yes, there is pain, but Love does not think that very significant."

By the end of the book, after a very long and trying journey filled with trials, such as traveling through hot deserts, deep dark valleys, walking on the edges of cliffs, and climbing steep, jagged mountain walls, Much-Afraid reaches the top. It is there that she finds that the flower of Love has bloomed in her heart and it is when the Shepherd gives her a new name, Grace and Glory, for she no longer was consumed with fear. He also gives her what He promised before the journey began—a beautiful smile and perfectly formed legs. She became a woman of beauty inside and out.

    Right around the time I finished reading the book I received a vision from God while in prayer. It was quite amazing even as I think of it today, and it is linked with the book. The vision was of the most beautiful rose. As I went to kiss it, thorns suddenly appeared. I shrunk back abruptly from kissing the rose. I then thought about it. *"Do I want to kiss this rose and endure the pain of the thorns?"* I decided, *"Yes, I will kiss the rose and it will be bittersweet—but the sweetness will be greater than the bitterness."*

    When I wrote about this vision in my journal, I entitled it "A Bittersweet Kiss." What the vision meant to me is that God was letting me know that I was going to suffer pain, but that there would be a sweet part to it. He wouldn't give me more than I can handle and He would be right there with me, loving me in the midst.

    A little later that evening I thought about the book and how the vision reminded me of a section within it where the Shepherd offers to plant the seed of Love in Much-Afraid's heart.

"Here is the seed of Love Much-Afraid,' said the Shepherd. But when she looked at it, it was a long, sharply-pointed thorn. Much-Afraid shrunk back. She then asked the Shepherd, 'Won't it hurt if you put it into my heart?' He just told her to repeat these words, 'When the seed of Love is planted in my heart, then I will love in return.' Then she told the Shepherd, 'Please plant the seed here in my heart.'"

The Shepherd did so, and it did cause a piercing pain, but then "suddenly, a sweetness she had never felt or imagined before tingled through her. It was bittersweet, but the sweetness was the stronger." Reading these words confirmed to me the vision that God gave me. It was another reason to trust God as He led me through the healing journey.

While on the journey of my healing process, I realized the importance of what God was showing me through this book. In order for Him to bless me with a man to love and be loved by, as I so often begged, pleaded, and cried to Him for, I needed to be healed. My heart was too wounded and I lacked the ability to love as God calls us to love in the relationship of a marriage. I could also relate to the fact that Much-Afraid had many traits about herself that she knew needed changing and she realized she didn't have the strength to make the changes on her own. She knew she had to rely on the Shepherd.

Another element in the book that was a help to me was the fact that Much-Afraid had to struggle through a long, hard, often painful journey, and I related to her trials as I dealt with mine. I also learned from the way she dealt with and overcame those trials as she listened to the advice and wisdom given by the Shepherd.

So God brought me to the place of healing. This is what He willed for me, and I accepted His will. I can tell you that it was worth it. Just as Much-Afraid's heart bloomed with a beautiful flower that represented Love, God made a flower of love bloom in me. Many years following my journey of healing, I sat down to paint an oil painting. The results are of a vibrant, red rose in full bloom. I was surprised at the results—the beauty of it. God showed me that He thinks that *I* am a beautiful flower; it is what I have become through His grace.

I received a confirmation on this thought from an old friend. I bumped into this friend only a year ago. We hadn't seen each other in twenty years since we attended prayer meetings together in 1989. After bumping into one another she sent me an email that read, "Holly, you have become like a beautiful flower. You give off such a beautiful fragrance to all who meet you." She admitted to me that when she knew me all those years ago, she didn't like me very much. She used to have to ask God for grace just to be kind to me. So you see...God changed me and made me beautiful, just as the Shepherd did to Much-Afraid.

God used one more visual and tangible object to speak to me of how He sees me. In the midst of my healing, while still at The Little Flower Home, a friend came to visit me. She had carrying in her arms a large box. She explained to me as she opened it that she needed to sell some of her collection of porcelain dolls in order to pay her bills. When she got the box opened, I peered in to see a beautiful two and a half foot Franklin Mint porcelain doll. She paid three hundred dollars and was asking for one hundred, twenty five. I bought the doll from her only because I knew she needed the money.

Later that evening however, I realized that God arranged the whole deal. God wanted me to have that doll so to remind me of how he sees me. While in prayer, God gave me a scripture found in Psalm 45:10,11 which reads, "Hearken O daughter and incline your ear; forget also your own people, and your father's house; so shall the King greatly desire your
beauty...the King's daughter all glorious within."

God, the King, was telling me—His daughter, that as I gazed on the beauty of the porcelain doll, that was how He saw me. Remarkably, I found that same scripture in the book of "Hinds' Feet on High

Places." Toward the end of the book, shortly after Much-Afraid arrived on the High Places, the Shepherd spoke those exact words to her. I decided to name my doll Grace and Glory, the new name given to Much Afraid, as a reminder of how God healed my wounded heart and transformed me into something beautiful.

Chapter Seven

I am listening intently to my counselor as she tells me that I have anger pressed down into the depths of my being, but I try to pretend it doesn't exist. She likens it to a garbage can—how when it gets to be full, we push the garbage down and try to keep it contained by placing the lid on it.

However, as garbage keeps getting stuffed inside, it begins to overflow out from under the lid and falls to the ground. "Your anger, as well as other negative feelings, is like garbage that you keep stuffing down, but it comes out in other forms, such as in your depression," she explained to me.

When a child is reared in an environment that is filled with violence, aggression, hatred and abuse, and reared by parents who lack the ability to love him, he most always displays the ugliness of his childhood as an adult. He will be unable to give to another true unconditional love, whether it is his own child or his spouse. If one is walking their journey with God, He will inevitably bring him to the place of healing; where God removes the garbage that is present deep within his heart so that God's beauty and love can dwell and pour out into others.

Following the evening of the prayer meeting, where God opened my eyes to the incest, I immediately found a Christian counselor. I knew that I could not deal with my past alone. I met with Janice for two and a half years once a week. My sessions with Janice were intense and inspired by God.

We opened each session with prayer, and invited God to shine His light and reveal the things that He willed. And because we asked, He had His way. He most always brought out something that I hadn't intended on sharing, or that I didn't even have knowledge of prior to that day. I discovered how creative God was when he made us, such as when He created the human psyche with its survival mechanisms. We ended each session with prayer, asking God to heal the area that we focused on, and to bring His peace into my heart. My healing process went swiftly. I believe it was because of my willingness, as well as the fact that we invited God to direct the sessions and use His power to do the healing.

It was in these sessions that God had lifted the top off of the garbage can—which was my inner being. It was filled with garbage that I had been stuffing down for twenty-six years. The fragrance that emanated from me was not like that of a rose. Repeatedly through the years, garbage would seep out into my life and into my relationships, but I would repeatedly stuff it all back down and shove the lid on as tight as I could. Now, the top had been removed. It was all there…the neglect, abandonment, the emotional and sexual abuse.

During these sessions, I relived the sexual abuse from my father. I felt and behaved as if it were occurring in the present. This was a good thing because I was able to respond and express my feelings the way that I should've responded when the abuse actually happened, but couldn't. I would see pictures in my mind—but never my father's face. I would see myself as a child. I would see large hands. They were evil! I was afraid of hands!

Over time, and still without picture memories, God revealed to me that my father sexually abused me as a baby. I've heard of people using the term "tissue memories." I would say that this term best describes what I've experienced. God enabled me to feel the feelings that were attached to the experiences. He also revealed things to me in other ways, such as when people prayed over me. God revealed truths to them about me through visions or knowledge that was revealed to them by the Holy Spirit.

Another method came through relating deeply to others' testimonies of abuse that I read about or heard. Every now and then I would read an account of another girl's testimony of abuse and it would bring me to an abrupt halt and cause me to sob uncontrollably. I knew that it had happened to me. It hit me in the core of my being.

Another way that God revealed things to me was through my dreams. It seemed that it was easier for my psyche to deal with things in my dreams verses while awake. My counselor advised that I keep a journal, which I used whenever I felt the need to express myself. I also used it to record my dreams. If I woke up in the morning and remembered my dream(s), I wrote them down immediately. This was very helpful in understanding what my dreams meant, which always led me to understand how I was feeling in the subconscious realm. When I didn't understand something in my dream, I asked God, and He always revealed the meaning to me.

During my healing process, God had brought family members to me to share their stories involving my father's abusive ways. This helped to validate me and my beliefs concerning my father. There were several stories that described my father's sexual misconduct throughout the years which involved his cousins, a neighborhood teen, and affairs with women.

There were other incidents of sexual abuse in my life that God had to heal, other than my father and brother. If you combined all the incidents not including my father, they do not even come close to the amount of pain that the abuse from my father caused. After doing public speaking to groups of women on the subject of sexual abuse, it is uncanny how many women share that they have had multiple incidents with various people throughout their lives. It makes me wonder about the reason for this occurrence. It's as if a door was opened with the first offender, and it stays open for other offenders to enter.

When I was a young girl about the age of five, my great-grandfather on my mother's side took me for a leisurely walk near his country home. It started out as an innocent stroll, but turned out to be the evil plan of my grandfather's to satisfy his sexual desires. He took me to a neighboring house which belonged to a relative who had passed, leaving it vacant. It was in this place that at this tender young age that my virginity was stolen. Stolen by another family member who was supposed to protect, care for and love me.

I was traumatized by this but I never told a soul. Following this dark day, the effects of my sick heart manifested in my physical body. I became a very sickly child; had many nightmares that caused me to wake up screaming; and I also became deathly afraid of going to doctors and dentists. If my mother told me ahead of time that we were going to a doctor or dentist appointment, I would lock myself in the bathroom and not come out.

On one occasion I fainted while at an appointment and at another time I vomited while waiting for them to call my name. I believe that I feared laying back in a dentist's chair or on an examining table because it made me feel vulnerable and trapped. It triggered my memory of having my great-grandfather on top of me. I reckon that this is the reason why as an adult I became very controlling of others, things and situations. This is just one example of the "baggage" that I carried into my relationships because of the abuse I experienced as a child.

Later on during my healing process, I would again experience anxiety when in tight places. I had extreme anxiety if I found myself in an elevator or in a small office with a man. In the latter situation, I would make an effort to keep the door open.

There were a few more incidents of sexual abuse in my life. When I was around eleven years old, I became a babysitter. On one occasion, the father of the child I babysat, tried hitting on me. He very casually got me cornered against the wall while we were in conversation and flashed me a seductive look. I responded by pulling away from him. On another occasion, the same man exposed himself. He nonchalantly sat down on the couch, and as he did, I got quite an eye full. He apparently wasn't wearing underwear because he hung right out of his shorts. I was creeped out, but at the time I wasn't certain that it was intentional.

There was a third incident concerning this man which occurred on an evening when I slept over in the guest bedroom. He and his wife thought it would be best for me to stay the night because they were coming home late. As I lay sleeping in the dark, I was awakened by a sound. It was the man tip-toeing into my bedroom. I saw his dark silhouette slowly and quietly approach my bed, but he couldn't see that I was awake. I was petrified! I decided to move around as if I were waking up and thankfully at that, he fled out of the room. I drew a deep sigh of relief and then vowed to never babysit for that family again.

The last incident of abuse happened when I was seventeen years old, while visiting my mother for the summer. My mother and Carl went away for the weekend so my sisters and I decided to have a few friends over. Before all of our guests arrived, I had finished a pint of hard liquor. I was so drunk that I went and passed out on my mother's bed.

Later, in the early hours of the morning, I was woken by the boyfriend of my sister's friend. He was on top of me having his fun. I admit that I didn't fight him off of me and it wasn't because I liked it. I just lay there…like a doll. Dolls have no thoughts, no feelings, no opinions. It was a persona that I was familiar with—a survival mechanism derived in my early years.

I know for a fact that I in no way led this man on. I had just met him and his girlfriend and barely spoke with them at all. The next day, my sister's friend told her that her boyfriend slept with me and it was because he wanted to make her jealous. He of course, made it sound like I was a willing participant.

The truth is that I was not a willing participant. The truth is that I was raped. There was no visible violence and there were no exterior scars. They existed nonetheless— inside my heart.

One more deep dark secret to add to the rest.

As part of my healing process, I feel that God desired for me to confront my family members. I don't think it is always necessary for a survivor to do this, but I felt that there came a time when God was drawing me to this place of confrontation, particularly with my father and brother. A little while later, I came to confront my mother on the issue of neglect. The first person I confronted was my father. It was the hardest thing I've ever done! I had so much fear inside of me. I felt so afraid of my father, even though I didn't have reason to be afraid of him at this point in time. I believe it stemmed from my childhood.

My father lived in New Hampshire and I in Rhode Island, so I had planned on confronting him on the phone. However, I think that if he lived five minutes away, I still wouldn't have had the guts to confront him to his face, and if I did, I believe I would've barfed in his face due to anxiety. During this period, I suffered from Post Traumatic Stress syndrome, and thus had a lot of emotional and physical impairments. As I said, I felt that God was calling me to do this, so I forged ahead as difficult as it was for me.

I had planned the day and time that I would call my father and prepared him to be available for my call. I took many steps to preparing myself for this moment. I had my boyfriend Dan, who was my biggest support throughout my healing process, right by my side. Dan, my counselor Janice, and I prayed for days leading up to the confrontation.

On the morning of the day, I woke up with a song in my head. This is a common form of communication that God uses to speak to me; through songs in the night, and they usually are telling me something about the day to come. The song is by the Beatles, and the words I heard were, "Blackbird singing in the dead of night. Take these broken wings and learn to fly. All your life, you were only waiting for this moment to arrive…to be free. Blackbird, FLY."

Wow! Those words are so profound, and they really touched me at that time, as they still do to this day.

I had written down the things that I wanted to say to my father. I made the call while Dan sat in the next room praying for me. I told my father that I had repressed memories that had come out and they were of him sexually abusing me. He didn't respond as if he was shocked, nor did he sound angry or accuse me of saying something outrageous. He also didn't ask me any details. I told him I was seeing a counselor and that we felt it best that I confront him. My father didn't deny my accusation, but neither did he admit to it. He responded with, "Is that so?"

I don't remember how we left things before we hung up the phone, but the following day I do remember. His wife Donna had called me and she knew what I had accused my father of. She said that he had told her everything. He also told her that my counselor had filled my head with nonsense. My father had his deceitful plan in motion that would make him appear innocent. I had no intention of telling Donna or any of his family members. Donna had told me that she told my father's sister with whom she was close friends because she had to share her burden with someone. Now two other people knew this dark secret.

On the phone, Donna asked me details of which I shared with her. She appeared to listen and take it all in. Following our phone call I felt she believed me because she didn't ask any questions that appeared as if she doubted me. She wanted to meet me face to face and inquire some more, so we made a date.

When we did meet, she asked for every minute detail, but I couldn't give them to her. I couldn't tell her *when* it happened, *where* it happened, or even *what* happened. At this early date of my healing process, I was not even sure what my father had done. I had no picture memories. Still, Donna didn't come across as if she doubted me. It was difficult for us both because we were really close friends. The next time I spoke with her on the phone, it was clear that she had chosen the road of denial. Since that point in our relationship, we have not been close.

I also lost the relationship I had with my aunt who knew of my accusation. This woman was my favorite aunt, the one whom I had taken after, and with whom I had a close relationship with. She also chose to live in denial. Aunt Mary at two different times threatened me to not tell my grandmother. I had never brought up the subject with her, but she was sure to get her point across on the matter. I felt that she was bitter and cold from the way that she spoke to me. My accusation now severed two relationships with my loved ones. It was very difficult for me to bear.

What was more difficult to bear was my beloved Nana and how she became hurt by the goings-on. I never, ever thought to tell my grandmother. I loved her too much to hurt her. But as my grandmother noticed that I did not want to come around on the holidays when my father would be visiting, she became troubled. She would constantly badger me on what he had done that I couldn't forgive him and be reconciled. She would call me on the phone with an angry, impatient tone in her voice, practically begging me to tell her what he had done. She always reminded me that Jesus calls us to forgive one another and if I really considered myself a Christian then I would forgive my father.

I couldn't tell her that on the times that I bumped into him at her house I felt physically ill. I would feel like I was going to vomit. I would also get weak in the knees and feel like I was going to faint. I would have to lie down and then leave early, saying that I was coming down with something. I then would go home and sob for hours until I fell asleep, only to have to face nightmares which would last for at least a week following the visit.

I've noticed a pattern in my family members of my father's side. Denial runs deep and wide. I've learned to really despise this trait that I often see people or families use. I suppose it is a legitimate survival mechanism but it simply pisses me off. Personally, I'd rather "Take the bull by the horns!" My opinion is, "Deal with it and then be done with it." Even though I never did tell my Nana what my father did, I clearly could see that she also chose to live in denial. There were so many immoral, bad deeds over the years that my father was known to do, but in her eyes he was the perfect son. If anyone ever tried to tell her different, she'd just as soon tell them to "Get lost."

While in the midst of the healing process, my mother came to stay with me when my sister was in the hospital. On one of those evenings in my apartment she overheard me crying. When she approached me to ask me why I was crying, I couldn't even stop crying to answer. Later, I sat down with her and told her what was going on in my life, that Dad had sexually abused me.

Mom didn't question me for a second. She didn't ask about the details as if I had to prove it to her. She was quiet, calm, and behaved as if she believed everything I told her. She didn't admit to having knowledge of it and I didn't get the feeling that she had. I got the feeling that she believed me so readily because she knew the immoral habits of my father and felt it possible that he would do such a thing. I never did feel angry towards my mother or put any blame on her. I am grateful that she left my father when she did.

Within a week of confronting my father, I did the same with my brother Michael who lived in California. I called him on the phone and told him that I confronted our father for sexually abusing me. He said that he couldn't recall if it ever happened to him, but there had been times when he wondered about it. I then confronted him for abusing me. He admitted also doing it to my sister, but he said, "That's normal kid behavior. All kids try things like that."

However, a year later while my brother was visiting RI, he once more broached the subject, only this time it was with remorse. Michael had apologized for hurting me and also my sister, although I don't know if he ever apologized to her face. He said that he didn't mean to hurt us.

That same evening, Michael and I we were traveling in my car when a Christian song came on called "Justice to Mercy," by Susan Ashton. As he listened to the words about forgiveness, he began weeping profusely. He was a grown man about the age of thirty, but he sat and wept as a child. This day with my brother brought resolution and a peace in my relationship with him. All of my years growing up I hated him, but for once, I felt peace in my heart towards him.

My sister found out what I had accused my father of and when we talked on the issue, she said she couldn't remember anything ever happening with our father or brother. Many people who have been sexually abused as children have no conscious knowledge of such, due to the repression of memories. Often the memories surface around the age of forty and are triggered by an incident associated with sexual abuse. For others, the memories never surface throughout a life time, but the effects of the abuse certainly do.

If a person had asked me at the age of twenty-four if I had been a victim of incest and my father the offender, I would've answered, "No way." Today, it's as if I can see the symptoms or signs a mile away in a victim. They may not have the knowledge themselves, but their behaviors tell the story.

A few years later I confronted my mother on the ways that I felt she had neglected me and my siblings. It happened when my mother made another visit to RI, on a day when she accompanied me to church. When the service ended, we remained in our seats and somehow got to talking on this subject. I very lovingly began to tell her of all the things that I wish she had done and all of the things that I wish she hadn't. All of my hurts came flowing out of me, which she received graciously.

I shared with Mom that my biggest hurt and disappointment was that she never bonded with me, even as a baby. She didn't hold me close and nurture me with her love, as moms are supposed to do with their new-born babies. I was shipped off to babysitters who did all that she was supposed to do; all that I longed for her to do. A child craves the attention and affections of her mother. It is what validates her and makes her feel lovable and valuable.

I so appreciated my mom's willingness to listen to me as I poured out my heart. It showed me that she cared about me and my feelings. She acknowledged my feelings verbally and apologized for everything. From that day on, I felt that she made a conscious effort to make amends. It was like balsam to my heart. From that day forward, my mother and I began to form a mother and daughter relationship, one which had never existed, not from the day she brought me into the world.

Confronting my mother was such a healthy thing for me to do. Prior to that moment, I had held bitterness and resentment towards my mother. I often would share very negative comments about my mother to others. My siblings and I often went on a tangent speaking about how our mother did so and so, and what a bad mother she was. We would get all riled up, letting the anger from the past fill our present. It was negative, ugly talk that only feeds an attitude of self-pity and depression. Once I was able to share my feelings with my mother, all of the negative feelings from the past dissipated, just as it had with my brother.

Confronting my father was also a healthy thing for me, even though he didn't acknowledge his offense to me. When I was able to accuse my father, it took the blame off of me. Victims quite often feel that they are to blame and are filled with shame. Also, by confronting my father, I was standing up for myself. I was saying, "What you did to me was wrong and I am no longer going to help you keep your sin a secret. I was an innocent child and you violated me."

Even though I was filled with intense fear at the time, and didn't feel very strong, it was empowering for me. I also brought out into the light something that was hidden in the darkness, thus releasing its power over me. Alleluia! Freedom…such as that of the black bird…"You were only waiting for this moment to be free…Black bird fly."

Chapter Eight

This evil man snatches me from the street and the next place I find myself is in a dark and dreary pit, way below street level. I am scrunched into a corner, backed in by these grotesquely-looking evil beings. There are several of them, and they take turns sticking their evil faces in my face as a means of taunting me. They succeed because I am petrified.

As I try to think of a way out of my dilemma, I begin yelling "Jesus!" Every time an evil being comes near me to scare me, I yell, "Jesus!" This makes the evil beings draw back, as if they are the ones who are afraid. And then suddenly, I am being lifted up, higher and higher, out of the dark pit and into the light. Now I am flying through the air, above buildings and trees, as if I have the wings of an eagle.

It took one year. Of course, there was to be more healing to come, but to a much lesser degree. From the time I left my job at The Little Flower Home, to the time I went back to work, totaled one year.

In the midst of my healing process I began having nightmares on a daily basis, sometimes having five of them in a single night. The sleepless nights caused insomnia in the evening and fatigue in the day. Slowly my nerves began to give way. Sometimes my body would just give out and I'd drop to the floor, which happened several times. My whole being just needed to stop. It happened at places such as in the aisle of Stop & Shop, the Showcase movie theatre, and at church.

My body also began twitching from head to toe. Over time, the twitching became more frequent and more aggressive. It happened twenty-four hours a day and became very noticeable. Meanwhile, I was still living and working at The Little Flower Home. Sometimes while working I'd just break down and sob uncontrollably. I had worked for a year in this pro-life ministry, but came to the decision that I needed to resign so that I could give my body the rest and care it needed.

Within the year that I was unable to work, God took care of me so wonderfully. He provided my every need to the detail. Leaving my job at the home meant losing my own home. Where was I to go with little money and no home? I remembered that Taunt was currently staying at her Florida home, which meant her in-law apartment in RI was empty. My aunt agreed to let me stay there for the winter and pay just a small amount of rent. It was the perfect arrangement for me.

During this period, I did very few things to fill my time. I was very limited as to what I could do because my mind and my body were weak. I have often used the term ill. I did not act as a person with a mental illness; it was just that my mind was tired. I couldn't think very well, and I could get overwhelmed very easily. I needed things to be simple. I needed to drop out of the social scene, which was mostly made up of friends from church. I was part of a large circle, about twenty of us, and we did everything together. I ended up spending much of my time in bed due to the fact that I suffered insomnia and fatigue. The two things that I made a point to do were to go to church, which included daily Mass, and weekly counseling.

The one person that I did spend time with was Dan. Dan was to become my husband in the years to come. I felt safe with Dan. He didn't pressure me to have sexual relations with him. He showed respect and dignity toward me. He was honest, humble, and down to earth. He also loved God and enjoyed praying with me. During my illness, Dan was a great help to me. He was there whenever I was in need, such as when I was too weak to go grocery shopping or to cook myself a meal.

One day I was at home and trying so hard to pray, but to no avail. I couldn't form the words in my mind. I called Dan up crying about it and he came right over and prayed for me. Another time I was trying to read a book, but I just couldn't. I would get so frustrated that I would cry. Dan would come and read for me. I had some close friends who over time gave up on me. They wanted me to be well. They would say, "Come on Holly. Get over it already. Forget about the past and get on with your life." I figured that they were tired of being sad right along side of me. I stopped answering my phone for this reason. I just couldn't act happy. And I couldn't act as if I cared about what was going on their lives because I was too consumed with my own.

Another way that Dan was a help to me was he showed me ways that I could release my anger. It seems that it is harder for women to express anger, and more acceptable for men. Women often feel that they have to be kind and submissive even when they are angry. Consequently, they are prone to having depression because they feel that they must repress their anger. Men, on the other hand, are prone to fits of rage because they feel free to express their anger. It was incredibly hard for me to even acknowledge that I had anger. It took a long time for my therapist to succeed in getting me to feel my anger. God showed me that I feared being like my father who expressed rage regularly and reminded me of an evil monster.

Eventually, I learned there was a ton of anger that was pushed real deep inside of me. When I did feel this emotion, I felt like I would lose control. It was scary! I didn't know what to do to release it—but Dan did. One night as we sat in his room hanging out, I wrote down the words, "I want to die." He said in reply, "Let's go for a ride." It was late and there was snow on the ground.

We drove for quite a while down Route 95 until he pulled off the highway and stopped under the overpass. He got out, stood under the highway and started yelling. I watched him for a while, then got out of the car and followed suit. He turned around, got back in the car and just waited for me to do what he knew I needed to do. It sure did feel good!

On another evening Dan took me behind a shopping plaza. He just happened to have canned goods in his car which he took and started throwing at the wall of the building. I got out of the car and he handed me the cans to do the same. It felt good to throw the cans with all of my might and to see them smash against the wall and watch the juice and vegetables fly through the air. Of course, I imagined the cans to be my father.

Other things that I did to release my anger were to write my feelings in a journal, punch pillows, and burn pictures of my father. Sometimes I would put a picture of my father on my bed and then pound at the picture with a baseball bat. Releasing my anger in a way so as not to hurt myself or another, was real important. If I hadn't, the anger would've consumed me. I believe that this was the reason why I had said that I wanted to die.

On the evening that Dan took me for that first drive, something happened within me. It was the first time I ever considered myself a victim. I thought to myself, "I am a victim." This was a big deal for me. It was as if with my acknowledgment of the fact, I came to accept it. This thought reminds me of the alcoholic who must first come to acknowledge that he is indeed an alcoholic, in order to work toward sobriety. Over time I would come to the place where I would no longer consider myself a victim, but a survivor. Eventually I was able to shout out proudly, "I am a survivor!"

The pain I felt during this year was intense. I often would be reminded of all the ways prior to this year that God had brought to me the realization of the pain that His Son endured. This fact once again became very real to me while at a St. Charles prayer meeting.

There came a moment when I felt like I couldn't sit in my chair another moment. I felt like I had to get out; as if I was losing control. I got up, walked out of the hall and into the kitchen. There on the wall hung a crucifix about five feet tall. As I gazed on that cross I began to cry. I fell to my knees, stretched out my arms just like Jesus, and sobbed. I remember feeling like I knew the pain that He felt; the pain in His hands as the nails were hammered through his flesh and bones. It made me feel better to know that I was not alone in my pain. I felt an odd sense of comfort just from that thought.

God took care of my financial needs throughout the year. I never went a month without paying my rent on time. I remember the day that I received my first Temporary Disability Insurance check in the mail. Prior to that moment, I had been praying, "Lord, I have no money left. I have no idea how I am going to pay for my groceries this week or pay my rent. Help me." I remember jumping up and down and praising God when I opened up that piece of mail.

After six months when my TDI ran out, I was able to collect General Public Assistance. Here I was with a bachelor's degree and collecting welfare. I not only received food stamps, but when they ran out before the end of the month, I had to go and get more food from St. Vincent De Paul—the ministry that I had been working at for years, which serves the poor.

One thing that Dan and I did at this time, so as to give back to the ministry, was to do the shopping at the local food bank. Dan had a pickup truck, so together we did the weekly shopping. This made me feel good inside. The ministry also paid for my counseling and provided my health care through the doctor on staff. I am happy to say that once I was well again, I continued to work for this ministry for many years to come.

When my aunt returned for the summer months, I had to find a new place to live. I found a dingy three-room basement apartment to live in, costing three times more than what I was paying my aunt. It became very hard to pay my rent, but God got creative and made a way for me. Every time there was a large amount of rainfall, my apartment would flood. I remember one evening while reading in my bed, water suddenly came pouring through my bedroom window, just as if a dam had broken. What a scene! But there was a blessing in it. I called my landlord who came right over with his wet vacuum and sucked up the water. Every time this happened, he took fifty dollars off of my rent. I began praying for rain toward the end of each month.

During this year of healing, I was diagnosed with hypoglycemia, which means that my blood sugar was low. I feel that this condition surfaced due to the stress I had in my life. I had a severe case causing me to faint at times. On one occasion I became unconscious. It was the worse episode I ever had, causing me to fall to the floor and not be able to respond to the medics that came to my assistance. I could hear them but I couldn't make out what their words meant and was unable to respond. To manage this condition I had to carry a glucose meter to keep record of my sugar levels and had to follow a strict diabetic diet. I eventually learned to manage my sugar well, until the day when God took this illness from me altogether.

There were a few things that I did during this year that brought me some peace and joy. One of the things that I felt God prompted me to do was read the book of Psalms from the Bible. I found strength and comfort when I read the Psalms in which King David calls out to God for help in the midst of his trials and where He praises God for them. David was able to praise God because He trusted that God would "work things out for good for those who love Him," as is written in Romans 8:28.

I read the Psalms every day and found that peace and hope would fill my heart when I did. There was one particular Psalm that God used to minister to me. While in prayer one day, God gave me Psalm 131, entitled "Humble Trust in God." In this Psalm, God reaches out to His children as a mother does to her baby. It states in verse 2 "Like a weaned child on its mother's lap, so is my soul within me." I felt that God was telling me to entrust everything to Him; that He would take care of all of my needs so that I would be content as a weaned child. I came to dwell on this scripture often during this period of suffering. I asked God to give me the words in a song, and He did. It is a beautiful, calm, and soothing song that I often sing today, to my children, as a lullaby.

I also found tranquility when I visited Roger Williams Park. I went there at least once a week, year round and fed the ducks. I would walk around taking in the beautiful sights in nature, and then make a stop to observe and feed the ducks. I would sit down and just watch them as they gracefully glided on the water's surface. I was able to leave behind the goings-on in my own life when I focused on them.

One day I decided that I would paint the ducks. Art was something that I began doing at a very young age, and it was something that I did when I was troubled. I frequently sat at our kitchen table all through my childhood years where I would create pictures and escape my troubled world. I loved to use pastels. I would always create sunny, happy pictures—never how I felt, but how I wanted to feel; how I dreamed of feeling.

During my year of healing I produced two paintings which were done with watercolor. The first was of a pair of mallards, a male and female. When I gaze at this painting it brings me back to the tranquility that I found with the ducks at the park. The second painting is of a lighthouse which stands in the middle of a dark, stormy ocean. The light's rays are white, which shine to the right of the house, and red, which shine to the left. The lighthouse represents God, and the rays represent the blood and water which flowed from the side of Jesus as He hung on the cross. Over the years I continue to paint during times of crises. It is just one means of expressing myself, and where I find peace and rest.

Another escape for me is in music. This also began as a child. If I wasn't drawing, I was singing. I spent hours in my room singing songs. I would play my mother's albums and eight tracks on her players. Sometimes I would make my siblings listen to me sing as I pretended to put on a concert.

As an adult, I bumped into a woman whom I used to play with at Auntie's house. She said to me, "I remember when you would force us to listen to you sing songs. You would stand on the wall in Auntie's backyard as if you were standing on a stage. And I remember that you sang one song over and over again!" I had to think for a moment as to the song that she was talking about. I then remembered that I absolutely loved the song, "You and Me Against the World," by Helen Reddy.

At this adult age, I had to ask myself why, as a child, had I an affinity for that particular song. It is about a mother who is talking to her child about how she will protect her child. One line states, "Wasn't it nice to be around someone that you knew, someone who was big and strong and looking out for you?" I have surmised that I preferred to live in a dream world when I was drawing and singing. It gave me the opportunity to leave my world of mire, at least temporarily. This has been true for me even as an adult. I thank God for these passions of mine; gifts from Him to me.

As the year was concluding, I visited a friend who was a social worker and she suggested that I might try taking medication to try to help me get back on my feet. I prayed about it and talked with a few people, including the Christian doctor who worked at St. Vincent De Paul. I decided to give it a try. I was given an anti-depressant that also aids with sleeping. Immediately things began looking up. I began sleeping peacefully through the night and waking refreshed. The fatigue that I had felt for an entire year was gone.

Right around this same time, God gave me a new scripture to hold on to. He gave me Psalm 30:5, which says, "Weeping only endures for a night, and joy comes in the morning." I felt that God was telling me that it was "morning"—that my time of suffering was coming to an end. Simultaneously, I was planning on going on vacation to visit my mom in Florida, and had the feeling that it was going to be a pivotal time in my life.

While on vacation, I went to Mass daily and spent time in prayer in the small chapel of the church. One morning I awoke with the memory of a dream. This was not any ordinary dream however. This dream is one that I can remember to this day, as if it happened just last night. This dream was an awesome dream, and stands out above all of the dreams I've ever had. The details were described in the beginning of this chapter, where I told of flying as with the wings of an eagle. The dream concludes with me sitting at a table in a church where people kept coming in to see me. They wanted to know more about God. They reached out to me with tears in their eyes because they so longed to have what I had. This is where my dream ended.

I prayed to God asking Him what the dream meant. God gave me a scripture from Isaiah 40:31, "Those who wait on the Lord shall renew their strength; they shall lift their wings and mount up as eagles." As I read this scripture, I remembered that I had these words on a plaque hanging in my kitchen that Auntie had given me to encourage me during my hardship. Because of this dream, I knew that when I would return to RI, things were going to be better. And they were.

Psalm 30 entitled "Thanksgiving for Deliverance" had come to fruition in my life. Verses 2 and 3 state, "I praise you Lord, for you raised me up…I cried out to You and You healed me…You brought me up from Sheol (near death); You kept me from going down to the pit." The very last verses of 12 and 13 really stuck out at me, so I asked God to give them to me in a song. The song has a happy, upbeat rhythm, whose words say,

> "You changed my mourning into dancing. You took off my sackcloth and clothed me with gladness; that my soul might sing praise to You without ceasing. O Lord, my God, forever and ever will I give you thanks."

I returned home feeling refreshed. I thought that it would be best to wait a bit before going job hunting just to be sure I was ready. Within a few weeks I was feeling great. Now that I was well, I qualified for unemployment insurance. My plan was to apply for teaching jobs at the elementary level, so I mailed out a dozen resumes to local schools.

Within a week I received a phone call from one of the schools. I was the last person to be interviewed, and the least qualified, but I got the job!

Ironically, I knew the principal of the school because she happened to be my fifth grade teacher at St. Teresa's School in Providence. I honestly felt that God orchestrated the whole thing. I felt so blessed to have gotten a job so quickly, and doing exactly what I had set out to do. Once I started teaching my second grade class, I found such joy that I knew I was exactly where I belonged.

Life became normal again. God restored unto me everything I had lost. I moved into a nice apartment with a friend, taught my school kids, dated Dan, resumed old friendships, and continued counseling. It was a total of two and a half years of therapy before Janice and I agreed that I was ready to discontinue. There was just more thing left for God to restore, and He graciously did so without my even asking. God healed me of hypoglycemia.

About a year following my recovery, I went on a retreat with Spirit-filled Pat Turbitt from Turbitt Ministries. During the retreat, Pat went around the room laying hands on the women. When she came and laid her hands on me I dropped to the floor. As I lay on the floor feeling a deep peace, I felt a tingling sensation that went up and down my body, from my head to my toes and back again.

Following the retreat, I pondered what the experience meant. I came to the conclusion that God had healed me of my sugar condition. Slowly over time I began to give into my sweet tooth and found that it didn't make me feel ill. Within the years to follow I would be pregnant three times and not once experience gestational diabetes. Since my healing, to this day, at the age of forty-four, I have not had a sugar condition. Alleluia!

Chapter Nine

My friend said to me, "Tell me about your dreams." I only have one dream—one great desire. "Oh Lord, bless me that I may be a holy, loving wife and mother. Send me a Godly man, and enable us to raise holy, healthy, and happy children."

    I was waiting for God to answer my prayer, the one where He would send my future husband knocking on my door. This is exactly how Dan came into my life! God had answered my prayer on a September afternoon while I was praying in the chapel at The Little Flower Home. That first day we spent time talking and walking the picturesque grounds of the shrine where the Home was located. From that day forward, Dan came to visit me on a weekly basis when I would cook him dinner, and then afterwards, we'd walk the grounds and pray together.

    Four years passed from the day we met, when Dan proposed. Dan took me to a quaint ocean-side church where he got down on his knee and read to me three different Bible verses which referred to

God's explanation of marriage. He then asked me if I would be his wife. After the initial shock, I blurted out, "I want red roses at our wedding!" And he graciously agreed. I knew without a doubt that he loved me and treasured me, and I looked forward to being his wife.

Dan and I had nine months to prepare for our wedding. It should've been a happy time, but I started to feel very restless. Fear started to creep up inside of me, so much so that I knew I needed the help of a counselor. Laura, my new Christian counselor, was a big help to me. She helped me to discover the reason why I was so restless.

I was filled with fear—a fear of intimacy with Dan. It wasn't so much the intimacy of sexual relations, but in the fact that I would be completely surrendering myself to another person—especially a man. That meant I would have to trust in him completely, and that would put me in an absolutely vulnerable position. Within a few months I was at peace with my future plans, and Laura and I agreed to conclude my therapy.

Dan and I married in 1996, outdoors on the grounds where we began our courtship, The Shrine of The Little Flower. It was a beautiful August morning—a story-book wedding (except for the few moments of comic relief). There were a violinist and pianist playing classical music as the procession began with my three, young nieces floating down the aisle and tossing red-rose petals all about. They were like little cherubs dressed in cream-colored dresses, with daisies dotted through their long-braided tresses.

My handsome three year old nephew followed, sporting the smallest black tux I had ever seen. Billy began his lone procession carrying out the important task of carrying the rings, but in a moment of panic, ditched the plan to walk gingerly down the aisle, and made a mad dash toward my sister, my bride's maid, who stood beside Bonnie, my maid of honor.

I began my walk toward Dan wearing my beautiful, long-awaited "hope dress," with my mother and father on each side of me. What happened next is comical, and caused my bundle of nerves to relax. Halfway down the lengthy aisle, I realized that the sequins covering my lace-covered glove were caught on my mother's gown of lace, right where her breasts lay. As we continued to walk, we tried inconspicuously to eliminate the problem at hand. I admit that in the moment, I was filled with great stress, until minutes later, when it happened a second time while standing at the altar.

As my mother went to release me, we realized that we were stuck once again. The laughter within me, as well as the congregation, had bubbled up. Comic relief was an asset. It helped to relieve the stress I felt by the need to have a perfect wedding. I had no idea however, that there was more comic relief to come!

At the conclusion of the service, I had it all planned to present Dan with a gift. I had ordered live monarch butterflies with the intention of Dan opening the box in surprise and seeing the butterflies released into the sky. It didn't happen as I had planned however.

When Dan opened the box, there was no gush of beautiful butterflies floating through the air. I waited a moment, only to see five out of twenty slowly take to flight. The rest of the butterflies either dropped dead on the ground or struggled to flap their weary wings—but without success, and so they too, ended up on the ground. My nieces and nephew were thrilled because they jumped out of their seats and successfully began to catch the butterflies, as they had always dreamed to be able to do. The wedding party and congregation were in stitches as they viewed this circus scene.

I learned an important lesson that day. Never order live butterflies to be delivered by a poorly-ventilated, metal van that must travel all day in the hot August sun before reaching their destination.

Following the wedding reception, where I sang my love song to God, we headed on a boat to Rose Island in Newport. Dan and I were going to spend the first evening of our honeymoon at the famous, historical Rose Island Lighthouse, where we would have the entire island to ourselves.

The evening was magical—a dream come true. It began where we picnicked by the light of the sunset. The sky held such beautiful colors as the sun slowly sank down over the horizon that we were sure God was blessing us with a show meant just for us.

But God had more in store. By the time we finished our dinner, the sky began to bedazzle us with an extraordinary lightening storm. And lastly, for the encore, God gave us the view of a spectacular starry sky. God's twinkly little lights shone brightly amidst a completely dark night, as there was no electricity for miles.

To top off the evening, Dan presented me with a gift while staying in the lower level of the lighthouse, a living museum. This is a moment that I will never forget all the days of my life. Dan's gift was the most beautiful wedding gift a woman of God could ask for. He presented me with a large, heavy box, which I curiously watched him carry onto the boat and across the bay. I anxiously opened the box that was meant for this special moment, and inside, found an antique pitcher and bowl.

Dan explained that he wanted to replace the one that was passed down to me by my great-grandmother, but was stolen from the basement of my old apartment. That in itself was very thoughtful, but what he did with it was even more incredible. He filled the pitcher with water and placed it by my feet. He then read to me the story from the Bible of how Jesus washed the disciples' feet. Through this action, Jesus gave an example of how He calls us to be humble and take the position of one who serves.

Like Jesus, Dan proceeded to wash my feet. As I watched in awe as he dried my feet, I had to dry the tears that spilled onto my face. Through his action, I understood that he desired to serve me all the days of our lives together. As I lay my head on my pillow that evening, I felt like the luckiest woman in the world.

Dan and I practiced natural family planning as the Catholic Church requires, thinking it might be best to wait a bit before having children. Even so, we had ourselves a "honeymoon baby." At this time, Dan and I decided that I would leave my job as a school teacher at St. Patrick's School to become a stay-at-home mom. I was very happy teaching my grade five children, and I think they were happy with having me as their teacher. But my greater desire was to be a mother, and to be the best mother that I could be. I was determined to be there for my children. I wanted to give my children all that I didn't have.

Dan and I were blessed in the fact that we could afford for me to stay home. I believe that God provided for our family because we were faithful and obedient to God's Word to tithe (give our first fruits to God, as found in Deuteronomy 14:22). Fr. Randall had encouraged his flock to obey God's command and to have faith that God would provide. It is an awesome testimony that within the eight years of our marriage, Dan's yearly income doubled.

I was thirty-one years old when we welcomed Gabriel in May of 1997. It was a joyous occasion! On a sad note, while in my first trimester, depression hit me. Depression, which seemed to become an issue during my year of healing, continued to rear its ugly head in the years to follow. One day while driving down the road, I had the thought of driving right into the Mack truck directly in front of me. Once I was in the second trimester, the depression abated, only to return postpartum.

During this time, Dan was a big help with Gabriel who was a colicky baby. When he was home, he spent a lot of time holding him, which seemed to be the only thing that would help Gabriel's discomfort. I'm sad to say that depression made me not want to hold him very much. This fact made me go back on anti-depressants, and once again they brought me relief.

After Gabriel arrived, our home got quite cramped. After all, our three-member family was now living in a small, second-level, bungalow apartment that I had moved into while single. We also learned that we were expecting our second child, at a time when Gabriel was seven months old. We were overjoyed at the thought of another child because Dan and I loved children. We began our search for the perfect home.

The closing to purchase our new home was set, and it was perfect timing. We were planning on moving into our new home right before Christmas. When the day came to sign the papers at the closing, the home owners had a change of heart. The wife decided she couldn't part with their home. That news was disappointing enough, but it got worse when we found out that the landlord of our apartment had already rented it out, and would not relent upon her agreement with the new renters.

It was sixteen days before Christmas! We had an eight month old baby, with one on the way, and we were to be homeless! We turned to God and prayed that we too wouldn't be forced to take up lodging in a stable like the holy family!

We searched frantically for an apartment or house, but to no avail. Finally, on the day before our eviction, our realtor found us an alternative. She found us a parsonage owned by a church that was temporarily vacant. We were given the home to rent for a total of three months until the future pastor would be moving in with his family. We were so grateful to God that He had taken care of our family. We moved into a large, beautiful country home, in the middle of a quaint small town, a half hour from the city.

Our Christmas was a special one because of its simplicity and because we were grateful to God for answering our prayers. It was simple because we lived mainly out of boxes. We knew we had to move within a few months so we didn't bother unpacking. Consequently, we had few Christmas decorations. As a matter of fact, our sole decoration was a manger scene.

That Christmas, Dan and I were forced to focus merely on the Christ Child, and we felt close to Him, as we shared a common experience—that of being exiled! When friends of ours from the city didn't visit because of the distance away, we often joked about how we were living in exile and would see them all again upon our return—God willing.

God did come through, but not before Dan and I received an eviction notice from the church because we were not out of the home on the given date. We had found ourselves a home, but oddly enough, we ended up in a similar situation with the home owners having second thoughts. This time we obtained an attorney and eventually we had our closing date. Alleluia! It all worked out in the end.

While still living in "exile," Dan and I had ourselves another scary situation. When I was five months pregnant, we went for an ultrasound and were told that our unborn baby had cysts on his brain. They told us that we needed to make an appointment for a Level Two ultrasound, which is more detailed, and we needed to meet with a genetic counselor. We immediately bombarded God with our prayers, and our family and friends at St. Charles joined us.

Upon meeting with a genetic counselor we were told that the cysts on our baby's brain usually meant one of two things: Our baby would not live long after birth, or our baby would have a serious disorder such as Down syndrome. The woman we spoke with even mentioned the fact that we might choose to terminate our baby. There was no way Dan and I were going to make that decision. We chose to put our baby in God's hands and prayed for a miracle. Only by God's grace were we able to turn this situation over to Him, and subsequently, lived with peace in our hearts as we awaited our baby's arrival.

When Christopher was born he appeared to be a healthy baby. When they did an ultrasound on his brain, the cysts were gone! Glory to God! He is faithful!

By the time Christopher arrived, we were living in our long-awaited, three bedroom home in North Providence. I was so happy to have my two boys, and so enjoyed nursing Christopher, which I did until he turned one. By the time Christopher was two and a half years old, I realized I had slipped into depression. I believe it may have been mild following his birth, but got worse with all of the sleepless nights I had, due to having two babies waking at all hours of the night.

When I look back at this period in my life, I view myself as a monster. I acted like a miserable person, often quick-tempered and harsh with my words. I was a mean person; mostly to my husband, and at times, to my precious babies. I behaved in a way that made me hate myself.

There came a day when I became aware of myself as if I were able to view myself from the outside, and what I saw made me want to die. In the next moment, I remembered that there was medication. With this thought came an image in my mind. I saw myself being in a dark hole, like an empty well, and looking up to an opening where I could see light. Through the opening, came a rope that reached down to me. I felt that medication was the answer and it gave me hope.

Within a few days something else happened that gave me hope. I was walking down the hall of my home from the living room to my kitchen and a prayer card came floating down upon me. I had no idea where it came from. There was no explanation that made sense to the human mind. It had to be supernatural. As I thought about this, it made me feel that God was looking out for me; that He knew what I had been going through and was giving me a way out.

Medication is often viewed as a bad thing. I understand the reasoning behind this thinking, but I am personally grateful for it. In the years to come, medication would continue to be a help to me and also to my son Christopher. As I prayed to God for help in certain situations, I believe that mediation was the answer He gave me.

Within a week of going back on anti-depressants my disposition improved greatly. I became more patient and tolerant of my husband's and children's faults, and I looked at life and others with a positive mindset. In this new, healthy state of mind, I was able to see objectively the way that I behaved prior to going back on medication. I came to realize that even though I acted horrible and mean, I wasn't that way inside my heart. I was a person with a chemical imbalance.

I also came to question why the people I loved and who professed to love me didn't see that I had a problem. It's as if they accepted me the way I was, like it was a natural way that I had always behaved. Inwardly, I was disappointed that no one, particularly my husband, came to me and said, "Something is wrong. The way you've been behaving is not like you. I think you need help."

I went to my mother and asked if on her visits to our home she noticed that I had depression. "I noticed that you were very on edge," she responded.

"Why didn't you say something to me Mom?" I asked. "I didn't want to offend you," was her sorry answer.

A part of me thought, *"What a waste of time, all those months living in a dark hole."*

I do believe however, that God allowed it and had His reasons. It was as if God had allowed me to walk through a dark valley, but I was not alone; He was with me the entire time.

I was always mindful of being the best wife and mother that I could be. However, I knew that I had to *learn* how to be a healthy, loving wife and mother because I never learned these things from my own mother. I was like a sponge seeking to absorb all that I could. Every morning at 8:00 a.m. for about eight years I listened to a Christian radio talk show, *Focus*

on the Family with Dr. James Dobson. I ordered tapes of shows and books that he spoke of and suggested. I continuously bought and read books about the "How to's" on mothering and being a godly wife.

I also went to daily Mass often during my marriage. I would bring the boys, and sometimes Dan would accompany us if we were going in the early morning. I very often felt that my goal of being a good wife and mother was unattainable. I failed so many times at behaving the way I knew I should. This is why I got myself and my babies out the door so to be at church for 7:00 a.m., to beg God for His grace. If I didn't get to church, I knelt down in my prayer corner in my bedroom—again, to beg God to help me fulfill my dream of being a holy, loving wife and mother.

There is a scripture that I often professed and claimed which is found in Psalm 91:14-16 NAS, "Because he (she) clings to me I will deliver him. I will set him on high because he acknowledges my name. He will call upon me and I will answer him. I will be with him in distress. I will deliver him and glorify him. With length of days I will gratify him and will show him my salvation." This verse was a comfort to me, and gave me hope.

Today, thirteen years later since the birth of my first son, amidst all those years of learning, I cannot for a moment boast about how I have perfected it. But I can say that I have never given up trying and praying to God for His grace to fulfill my dream, and my desire to please Him.

It has always been easier to love my children than to love my husband. I reckon it is because it wasn't children who wounded me as a child but men. Throughout my years of learning how to be the wife that God called me to be, I faced many mountains. Every few years I came across a block; something in me that was a block to loving my husband. At these times, I turned to a professional.

I remember my first appointment with a counselor since being married. I told her, "I hate the way that I act toward my husband. I behave in a way which is unkind, even hateful at times. Afterwards, as I realize my actions, I ask myself, '*Why? Why did I do that? Why did I say that?*'" I knew that I didn't behave as a Christian should, and as I reflected on my sins each night when I went to bed, I felt that I was such a sinner. I knew that my actions were not pleasing to God. God brought this particular issue with my husband to my attention one evening at a Charismatic prayer meeting with Don and Pat Turbitt.

On this one night, it was as if God again, made the scales fall from my eyes. I was able to see how I had been treating my husband. You could say that I was abusive towards him, emotionally and verbally. Nothing he did was ever good enough for me. I always seemed to focus on the things he failed to do or didn't do well. It was as if I was in a constant desire to fight with him and be at odds with him. During this prayer meeting, I was so convicted that I felt led to go before the church of two hundred people and confess my faults. I told everyone how God had convicted me, and as I did so, I broke down in tears and was barely able to speak.

As I left that meeting, I didn't feel sad. I felt liberated and grateful that God took the time to help me see my ways, and He did it in a way that wasn't condemning. As always, He was gentle and merciful in dealing with me. When I got home that evening, I sat Dan down and told him all that had happened. I confessed to him all of the ways in which I knew I mistreated him and asked for his forgiveness. Of course, he obliged. This knowledge was just the beginning. Unfortunately, I came to that same place of confession and forgiveness with Dan on several more occasions. I had the knowledge of my sin but was unable to stop committing it.

My excellent counselor Paulette was not only a skilled therapist, but she also surrendered to the wisdom and truth that the Holy Spirit gave her. One day she told me, "Holly, you have a bitter root, which is a hatred of men." I knew at that moment that she was right. As I thought about it, I came to realize that in the midst of all the fighting and my anger toward Dan, I frequently thought to myself, "*I hate him.*" I thought that thought almost on a daily basis. Every now and then as I thought those words, a part of me made an association with my father.

God showed me that my hatred towards men began while in the womb when my father abused my mother, and was validated by his abuse towards me, as well as by the other men who abused me later in my life. Subconsciously, I reflected these feelings onto all men, including my own husband, whom I had professed to love for many years. Paulette and I prayed for God to remove this bitter root, but it did not happen overnight. There was no supernatural moment where God in His power delivered me on the spot. The deliverance came months later, and it happened through forgiveness.

At this time in my life I felt that I had forgiven my father. I prayed for him and harbored no ill feelings towards him. I had Christian people tell me that it was OK to love my father from a distance. I didn't need to be in his life. For a time I felt that this was alright with God. But at this present time, I felt that God was saying, "*Holly, it is time to go deeper. I want you to love him on a daily basis with your words and your actions.*"

I had experienced turmoil within me just thinking of being in the same room with my father. In the past, I had felt physically ill in that circumstance. This would be the third time that God brought me to a place of going deeper in the process of forgiveness. This time would be the deepest and final time—the one that would transform me, deliver me, and free me.

The bitter root would be broken by my decision to love my father with all of my being, and to let go of all of the resentment that I had been holding on to. God had showed me that I was still holding on to it as if to punish my father. Only, it hadn't done anything in regards to my father. It was hurting me and my marriage.

It began on a women's retreat, when the leader Pat Turbitt, spoke on the topic of forgiveness which led me to think of my father. Following the talk, I randomly opened to God's Word where my eyes fell upon the scripture of 2 Corinthians 2:5-11 entitled, "Forgiveness for the Offender." In this scripture Paul encourages forgiveness towards an offender and to "reaffirm your love for him…anyone you forgive, I also forgive…I have forgiven in the sight of Christ for your sake in order that Satan might not outwit us."

The week I returned home from the retreat I found a Joyce Meyer magazine in my mail box. I had never heard of Joyce Meyer, preacher, evangelist, and author, until that moment. Inside the magazine was an article that she had written about how her father sexually abused her for years and how God called her to forgive him. Not only was she to forgive in her heart but she was prompted by God to take care of him in his elder years.

Joyce bought her mother and father a home, which was located in her own neighborhood. She tended to the needs of her father, all the while praying for his salvation. Eventually, she had the blessing of witnessing her father receive salvation, and got to baptize him in her own church.

God used Joyce's testimony to give me courage. I thought, *"If she can do it, then so can I."* I wavered a bit until I spoke to Pat Turbitt about it over the phone. She told me, "If you think that God is calling you to do this then you best obey Him, and don't hesitate." Her words hit home for me. I immediately wrote a letter to my father inviting him and Donna to our home for Christmas day dinner. My father had never been to my home, and had met my two boys only a handful of times while at my Nana's home.

My father accepted the invitation, and from that moment, until the day they arrived, I struggled interiorly. Whenever I thought of my father, two emotions welled up inside of me—FEAR and ANGER. If I had held on to those feelings, I most likely would have canceled our plans for Christmas. However, as I sought God and His will, He showed me that what I was feeling was not of Him. It was of the devil. I had to renounce those feelings. I began to claim scriptures such as, "Fear is useless. Trust is what is needed," and "Perfect love casts out all fear" (1 John 4:18). I also reminded myself that I had nothing to fear; that my father could not hurt me the way he did when I was a child.

Every time I felt anger towards my father, I asked God to help me to love him and to see him with His eyes. God began to fill me with compassion for my father. Instead of thinking, "*I hate him. Look what he's done to me!*" I started to think, "*I wonder what was done to him.*" A person isn't born with the tendency to sexually abuse others. It was very obvious that my father was a troubled and miserable man whose actions hurt others. I've heard Joyce Meyer say, "Hurting people hurt people."

As God filled me with compassion, He also gave me a revelation. He showed me something new in a popular and well known parable *The Prodigal Son*, found in Luke 15:20. In the parable it states, "While he (the son who squandered all of his money while living in sin) was still a long way off, his father saw him and was filled with compassion for him; he ran to his son, threw his arms around him and kissed him." God showed me that the father didn't wait for his son to admit his offenses and ask for his forgiveness.

Many people think that they are exempt from forgiving someone if their offender hasn't admitted their faults and apologized. In my case, my father had never admitted to sexually abusing me, hence neither had he asked for my forgiveness. Even so, God was telling me that I should forgive him and love him and to leave the judging to Him. I took to heart this scripture in Luke 6:37, "Stop judging and you will not be judged. Forgive and you will be forgiven."

I made up my mind that I was going to be an example of love to my father, and pray that my love for him would transform him. I thought, *"My loving him will show him that I forgive him, and will cause him to believe that God loves him too, even though he has sinned against God and his own daughter. My love will melt his hardened heart and give him the courage to turn to God in that vulnerable moment of repentance."*

I had these things in my heart as I opened our home to my father on that Christmas day. At the end of our visit and saying our goodbyes, I closed the door behind me. On that day, I literally closed the door to resentment and bitterness, and the lasting effects filled me with a deep peace. As Dan and I thought about the day, we realized that it surprisingly was a pleasant one. I myself realized that I had no negative feelings the entire day. I didn't have any of the symptoms such as feeling dizzy, weak in the knees, nausea, or the need to cry. I hadn't once felt anger or fear. I only felt peace.

Within the following weeks and months, I realized that I behaved differently towards Dan. I was a changed woman. Forgiveness freed me and delivered me. It enabled me to be the loving wife that I had prayed so often to be. God answered my prayer.

Chapter Ten

I look out into their little faces—some dirty, some shy, some brown, some yellow. I lead them in song in the hopes that they will be filled with the joy of the music, and of the message that my songs carry, "Jesus loves you...He loves little children...And He will make you happy with His love that fills your heart." If I make only one child smile, then I will leave here with a smile on my face and joy in my heart.

I felt a need to be something or someone other than Gabriel and Christopher's mom, and Dan's wife, so I found ways to use my talents outside these roles. Ten years after receiving my student-designed degree in Music and Theatre for Children, I found ways to once again delve into these passions. I applied my love of art and children while mentoring orphan girls, and my love of music by starting a business called Music with Miss Holly where I would introduce the world of music to young children.

I discovered that there lived a foster mother, a nun in our neighborhood. I learned that she took in girls who were in the state's custody. I thought it would be nice to spend time doing arts and crafts with the girls so I introduced myself to the nun. Sr. Jane and I became fast friends, just as the girls and I did. I began by visiting the girls once a week, but over time, my husband and I became much more involved.

Several times a year Sister took time to go on week-long retreats and during those times, I became the substitute foster-mom for the girls. There were times when Dan and I had four girls in addition to our two boys. We had a lot of fun with the girls. I was in my glory because I had very much desired to mother a girl.

Sister and the girls became like family to our family. We went on many camping trips together and other such fun excursions. Every now and then I would come to be attached to a girl and ask Dan if we could adopt her, but he thought it would be best to adopt when our boys got older. April was one of those girls. April became very special to us as she was with Sister for five years. Eventually, April got adopted at the age of thirteen. It wasn't until this past April that God brought her back into my life due to her need for shelter, as her parents through adoption forced her to leave upon her eighteenth birthday.

Once again I feel like a substitute mother to April. She is like a daughter to me, and I am gladly able to mentor her again as she is ushered into womanhood as an adult. I feel blessed to be in this role again with April, and marvel at the workings of God as He weaves the people and events through the tapestry of my life.

As my youngest was approaching Kindergarten, I knew I would have more time on my hands. I learned of Kindermusik, an international franchise where owners receive training and licensing to facilitate music classes in a small "mommy and me"

setting. I went through the three month computer-based training to receive my license, purchased several thousand dollars worth of percussion-type instruments, and the curricula required. I traveled with my program to day care centers, libraries and birthday parties until I later built a studio in our home. At that time, I branched off from Kindermusik to found Music with Miss Holly, where I would have much more freedom and could allow families with a small income to participate. This is something that I still do today after seven years, and it is a total joy for me.

Another place where I found joy and fulfillment was at St. Vincent De Paul Ministry. I had spent several years away from this ministry to focus on the rearing of my little ones, but returned when they entered grade school. This is the ministry that had assisted me in my time of need, and where I had also volunteered for many years prior to becoming a stay-at-home mom. It is an incredible inner city ministry which serves thirty thousand people a year. It is open five days a week, and provides many services to the underprivileged.

This ministry offers a weekly meal to three hundred people, a food pantry, clothing twice a week, and medical care. All of these services are free and are made possible strictly by donations and volunteers. I spent about ten years total in this ministry under the leadership of the director Cindy, the only paid staff person. During those ten years, I had many different positions such as secretary for the medical doctor, data entry for the director, food server/waitress, supervisor of the children's program and assisted the director in the running of the Christmas and Thanksgiving food basket programs.

Some of my most memorable times with the ministry were during the holidays when we put together food baskets. We spent the entire year gathering food for the baskets and had many churches that collected specific items just for this purpose. Come the week of the holiday, the church hall where the meal was given, would be filled to overflowing with the collected food. In addition to non-perishables, we had thousands of pounds of fresh vegetables that were donated by local farmers.

On one of the days of preparation, we spent the entire day categorizing and bagging the vegetables. Following is the picture in my mind that I will never forget. Imagine ten six-foot tables, each overflowing with vegetables, one which had potatoes and another butternut squash, and so on. However, there was such abundance that the vegetables were not only piled several feet high on the tops of the tables, but were also piled under the tables and two feet around. Each year we collected enough food to give a basket, (a two by three cardboard box) and turkey to approximately six hundred families.

Another treasured memory I have is seeing young grade-school students working hard to put the baskets together. While I was still teaching fifth grade students, I began the tradition of taking my class on a field trip to help put the baskets together. This was always my class's favorite field trip of the year. It was evident that they felt good about themselves because they were doing a kind deed for the sake of others. Eventually, Cindy the director invited many schools to participate so that today, during the basket-making week, one can visit and find dozens of young kids going about the business of giving back to the community. It has become a tradition in many of the surrounding schools.

Before I left the ministry the first time, I created and ran a program for children during the weekly meal kitchen. Cindy wanted to give the children a safe place to eat because they came together with about three hundred adults from the streets. We also wanted to give their parent(s) a break to enjoy a quiet meal without tending to their children.

I supervised a special meal made just for the children which was given in a separate room from the main eating hall. We began with saying a prayer of thanks for the meal, and then our goal was to befriend the children and make them feel special. We also tried to teach them proper behavior at the dinner table, as most of them lacked such knowledge. Once the children were finished eating, I took them to an adjoining room and did activities with them which focused on God. I sang songs such as "Joy in my Heart," and did a craft with them as well. I always gave them a "Jesus" sticker and a hug before they left. The program was a wonderful success.

I returned to the ministry because I felt that my life was lacking meaning, and knew that when I volunteered there, I felt fulfilled. I returned to run the children's program only to be surprised I wasn't dealing with children. When I left the ministry, I was serving young children at the average age of six, but now the average age was thirteen.

My first week back was quite a challenge. I had a group of rowdy, sarcastic, street-wise teens who made their fun by heckling me. When I left there the first week, I thought *"This is not what I signed up for, Lord."* But when the following weeks came, I felt God nudging me to return. It became a matter of obedience to God, because it really wasn't a fun or rewarding experience for me. I had to change the way I did things because of the age difference, so I brought in board games and playing cards. This was a great way to engage the teens. When it got warm outside, I took them to the parking lot where we played yard games such as paddle ball and Frisbee. Going to the ministry weekly was starting to be fun again, and over time I found it rewarding.

The more time I spent with the teens the better they behaved towards me. I came to know the regulars well. The group consisted of about seven teens, three of which were siblings. I began taking out one or two of the teens for a time of recreation. Only once did I take a group of them out, which was the last time I did that. When they were in a group they tended to want to act cool in front each other. During this outing at a movie, a few were throwing popcorn, while the others talked very loudly.

These teens didn't behave like model citizens. You could say they were troubled teens, and hence were quite difficult to handle. Nonetheless, I came to love these teens. I could empathize with them because I too was a troubled teen. These teens definitely didn't have it good at home. They were all from single-parent families and lived in poverty. Dinner for them was a bag of chips, a candy bar and a Coca Cola. The neighborhood they lived in was filled with crack houses, prostitution and monthly shootings.

Other outings included a visit to the zoo and the Museum of Science. These outings which were part of my own family, I did with the siblings in the group. I became friends with their mother Darla and like an "auntie" to the family. Because Darla trusted me, I often took her children, which included her toddler. I had her children visit at my home on a few occasions. One year the entire family came to our home to open Christmas presents.

Darla is just one example of a single parent who tried hard to be a good parent but lacked the skills. She also had a lot of her own issues which left her unable to care for the needs of her children. Each of her five children, but one, had a different father. The father of her youngest was living with them at the time that I knew them. He was a recent convict who was a live-in boyfriend and liked to beat on Darla when he was drunk.

I also took turns taking the teens clothes shopping over a period of a few months. These kids wore clothes that were two sizes too small or large, and were dirty, torn and out of fashion. I believe this was their favorite outing with me, which is probably the reason why they were on their very best behavior. I can remember seeing their faces light up with joy as they placed their new clothes in the shopping cart. It was quite rewarding for me.

A few years later, the teens seemed to outgrow the children's meal program so I didn't see much of them. The numbers started to dwindle in my department right around the same time I felt God nudging me to move toward the adult guests of the meal kitchen. My new goal was to befriend the adults and if possible, share the knowledge of God with them. Wherever I saw an empty seat I would sit down, introduce myself and try to connect with the guest.

Over time I came to gain the trust of many of our guests. They started to open up with me and tell me what was going on in their lives. I called them by name, and they called me Miss Holly. I guess they heard the kids call me by that name. I didn't mind it because I felt that it was an endearing term, as well as one that carries respect. Every now and then I did a little extra for a guest, one whom I'd gotten to know. Sometimes I gave a ride or a few dollars. Mostly, I gave a smile and a kind word or two, as a friend would.

    I became friends to several of the guests at the meal kitchen, as they were regulars who came for many years. I remember Matt who owned an apartment building, but lost his job and his house due to gambling. I called him "Cat Man" because he had about fifteen cats living with him, until the day he became homeless. Moe was highly intelligent, if not a genius. He knew something about everything. He didn't drink or take drugs as many of our guests did. I loved conversing with Matt because of our interesting conversations, but he was also a friendly and kind man. I don't know why it is that he stayed homeless for many years. He didn't speak of family though, as most of our guests didn't. It was as if they were alone in this world, without love and support.

    I can remember another friend named James, also kindhearted and intelligent. He too had no need for drugs or alcohol. He was on SSI and had an apartment through the state's housing program. I eventually discovered by talking with James that he came to the meal kitchen to talk with and make friends. He had food at home in his kitchen and spoke of cooking various meals, but he had no one at home to talk to and share a meal with.

    Another friend I met at the meal kitchen was Mickey. Mickey was a young man at the age of twenty. He lived in a crack house which was located just a few buildings down from the meal kitchen. Mickey not only had a drug problem but also a drinking problem. Sometimes he would try to commit suicide and on one of those occasions I went looking for him because I knew of his intentions.

Over time I got to know Mickey and when he was sober he desired to be free of his addictions. I got another friend who was male to assist me in helping Mickey. We began talking in depth with him and praying with him. One day when Mickey was sober, we brought him to a residential rehab where he stayed for a few weeks. We visited him regularly and brought him things, but this didn't last too long. On our last visit, we discovered that Mickey had given up on the rehab process before completion.

John is the friend that was in my life most recently. I got to know him in my last year of working in this ministry. John was a man about the age of thirty. He really seemed to have his act together. He was bright, witty, and was strong in the area of social skills. I loved conversing with John. He had a charisma about him that attracted me and the others around him. He also quoted scripture and spoke of God. In the beginning, I couldn't figure out why he was a guest in the meal kitchen. I never saw him high on anything.

John told me he was unemployed because he did seasonal construction work. I tried helping John gain employment. I brought him to our home and helped him put together a resume and research jobs online, as I had a computer and he didn't. On several weekends John took the bus to our home where my husband and I gave him odd jobs to do around the house to earn a little money. He was always kind and respectful to me and my family.

Eventually, I discovered John was an alcoholic. He did a good job hiding it from me for a very long time. Apparently, he was tired of hiding it, and the truth became known to me that his addiction is what consumed his time and energy, and was also the reason why he stayed unemployed and in need of the meal kitchen.

My experiences at the ministry inspired me to write an essay entitled "The Poor." In this essay I give a definition of the word, which is "to be lacking or to be in need." I discovered through my many friends at the meal kitchen that what they really lacked and what they were really in need of is LOVE. I state,

> "You may have a friend who shares a similar story, like the stories behind the faces of our poor. They are the stories of the Vietnam Veterans forever scarred because of their life experiences in the war...stories of the people suffering from undiagnosed mental disorders as severe as Schizophrenia...stories of the runaway teens who've escaped the neglect or abuses of their families...stories of abused and battered women, living a life similar to the ones they lived as children...stories of immigrants who've escaped all of these scenarios in their own countries, to settle here in a foreign land, knowing only a foreign tongue, without a penny to their name.
>
> The difference between your friend and the one who eats at the meal kitchen, is that your friend most likely has had the support of family or friends to carry him through the difficult times in life. He may have been given

financial support, and thus all of his temporal needs met. He may have had an education, which gave him confidence and knowledge which is needed to rise above the obstacles in life. Or maybe he had a loving mother always there for him day or night telling him everything was going to be all right, and that he wasn't alone. What a difference it makes to the human soul to know that he or she is loved and not alone. Thus, I believe the greatest need of the poor is LOVE."

I conclude my essay with the answer—where one is to find "LOVE." The answer is in God's Word. In 1 John 4:7,8 it states, "Love comes from God…God is love."

The founders of St. Vincent De Paul had this knowledge. They possessed God's love, and He put in their hearts His desire for them to reach out, not only to provide the needy with their basic needs of food and clothing, but also to provide the basic need of love.

This is the reason why three hundred people are considered "guests" when they walk in for a meal, and are waited on for an entire hour while being fed a three course meal with love and a smile. But the meal never begins without everyone bowing their heads and giving thanks to God first. So at St. Vincent De Paul, the guests are fed food to make their bodies strong, and the knowledge of God and His love to feed their spirits.

I feel proud and privileged that I was able to serve the poor (as is commanded in God's Word) at this outstanding ministry, and I will always treasure my memories and experiences from it.

Chapter Eleven

A woman whom I had never met comes up to me and gives me a piece of paper with words which she said she heard God say to her and are meant for me. She tells me of the vision that God gave her which accompanied His words. She saw me standing on the side of a road. I was looking ahead at the road noticing how it had many big bumps and deep potholes; it was also steep and had many sharp turns. She could sense that as I looked ahead on the road that I was to travel, I felt sad, alone, and overwhelmed. The words that she heard our Lord speak to me were, "Let Me take the wheel as you sit in the passenger's seat and let me drive."

Several years after our second son was born, my husband and I tried for another child. Getting pregnant was never hard for me so we succeeded on our first try. Within the first few weeks of my pregnancy I felt that God was telling me to name our baby Theresa. Then came the day I found out that our baby wasn't going to make it. Even after I lost my baby, I received confirmations from God that Theresa was the name He chose and so I knew that my baby was a girl. I wrote my good-bye in the journal I started when I realized that I had conceived a child. I have a journal for each of my children in which I write down my thoughts about them as they grow. I began each on the day that I discovered we were expecting.

About a year later Dan and I decided to try again. Bam! We were expecting. At five weeks, we got to see our baby's heart beating in an ultrasound! It really put my mind at ease, as I had such anxiety that we would lose this baby as well. As always, hearing or seeing our baby's heart beating was an amazing experience! It confirmed that new life was growing inside of me. How fortunate I felt to be God's instrument with which His miraculous power worked.

This time I felt God telling me that the baby's name was to be Grace. I knew that these names were from God. Because of this, I chose not to use the names that I already had in mind before marriage. Unfortunately, it wasn't meant for us to meet Grace here on earth. On the day that we lost Grace, I was surprised to see her tiny body with webbed feet and hands. It was a huge disappointment to lose another child.

Again, God gave me confirmations of our child's name. On a day that I had been grieving, I turned to God for comfort and strength. I was praying in a chapel with my eyes closed, as I poured my heart out to God. At one point I opened my eyes and happened to look up and see the word "Grace" on a plaque. As I left the chapel and drove off, I found myself driving behind a car with the bumper sticker, "Grace happens." I took these as signs from God of our daughter's name. Now I had two little girls living with God in heaven. Again, I shared my goodbye with our daughter and added to her journal the picture that we had gotten from the ultrasound.

It took a while to heal from my two miscarriages. After each one, I had said that I would never try again. I feared losing another and having to deal with the loss and pain all over again. They say that "time heals all wounds," and in this case it was true. Because my husband and I loved the thought of more children, we decided to try again. I was sure that God would not take another child. I prayed fervently and stood on my faith that God would answer my prayer. I remembered these words, "What father gives his son a snake when he asks for a fish?" (Matthew 7:10)

Again, it was in no time that we were expecting for a fifth time. I had many sleepless nights and much anxiety as I waited for the third month when most babies who make it at that point grow full term. We made it to the third month of the pregnancy and felt we were in the clear. I began to get more sleep at night, thinking that I would see the face of the baby growing in my womb. I began wearing maternity clothes and shopping for our new baby. I felt confident after seeing our baby through the ultrasound and hearing the heart beat on several occasions.

But it wasn't meant to be.

Faith, the name that God gave me, never made it. On my monthly checkup, I waited to hear the heartbeat, but to no avail. My two small boys were waiting with their expectant little ears to hear it also.

"Mama, where is it? I can't hear it?"

"Just a minute boys. She must be hiding from us."

The nurse brought us into another room where I met the ultrasound technician who proceeded to view my baby in the womb. As I watched her turn the monitor away from me so that I couldn't see my baby, I knew she was no longer with us. What a devastating moment! I didn't know what to say to my boys as they were still waiting to hear the heartbeat. I don't know how I made it home that day. It's all a blur.

I do remember however, when Dan finally made it home, early from a business trip. The moment he met me, I fainted. I awoke on the kitchen floor with him beside me. I wept in his arms while he held me and comforted me. All I could think of was that my womb was now a tomb. I had to carry our dead baby around for eight days until there was an opening for me to have her surgically removed.

I got through that horrible day by listening to praise and worship music. I asked my OB-GYN doctor whom I had known for years if I could keep my walkman during the surgery. He said that it was against hospital policy, but he made an exception for me. I left my home with the music playing in my ears and never took them out until I returned. I guess I was trying to escape the present, but did so by resting in the knowledge that I had to lean on God for His strength and comfort, as David did when he wrote the Psalms. David constantly praised God in the midst of his trials, believing that God would help him to prevail.

The following day, I wrote my good-byes to my third little girl, Faith.

"My dearest Faith, I miss you so much! I want you so much to be with me here so I can hold you and squeeze you. How hard it has been since your passing. I was so down, I didn't want to live…I look forward to the day when I will meet you in heaven! I love you Faith Marie. Your Mama."

Speaking of faith, I was trying hard to hold onto mine. Losing three babies sure was a test of faith. Much healing was needed at this point. Depression began to get the best of me. I began to desire to be in heaven with my girls and it was all that I could think of. I felt life would be better in heaven.

I know now how ridiculous my thinking was and that I had my boys who were still living and needed their mommy. But this is how depression can be. I actually believed my boys would do just fine without me. I see clearly now that these thoughts came from the pit of hell. I thankfully made the decision to increase the anti-depressants that I had been taking and within a week or two the despairing thoughts had dissipated.

I came to peace with the loss of my three girls when I went on another weekend-long women's retreat with Pat Turbitt. I remember how much grief I had that first evening. But by the final few hours of the retreat, I felt a peace that "passes all understanding" (Philippians 4:7). On the second day while in prayer, I shared my feelings with God. I told Him how much I wanted to see my girls or hold them for just a moment. It was so difficult to love my children from afar. I wanted something to hold on to as a remembrance. This thought came to me earlier in the day while at lunch, when I saw a picture that made me think of my three girls.

I was sitting next to a woman who had been taking things out of her purse and placing them on the table. Of those things, I happened to notice a small picture card that had three young, red-headed, curly-haired girls. They all looked about a year apart, which my miscarriages also were. My husband, his sister, and her two girls have red, wavy hair and his other sister has very curly hair. I had thought that my three girls probably would've looked much like the girls on the picture card. I shared with God that I was thinking of how nice it would be to have at least a picture of my girls to look at in remembrance.

Following my prayer with God, I toured a small Christian bookstore nearby. I was looking for that "something," hoping that God would lead me to a token of remembrance of my girls. I went straight to the rack that held small prayer cards. I was surprised to see the woman with the picture card whom I had met at lunch. I told her about the card I noticed she had and asked her where she had gotten it. She very graciously gave it to me to keep and I still have it today, seven years later, where it sits on my bureau in my bedroom.

By the third and final day of the retreat I had a peace and a joy in my heart. God may have taken my children to be with Him, but He gave me the strength to endure the loss, as well as heal my broken heart with His love. A few months later, He gave me another gift which again reassured me of His love.

At Christmas, God gave me another picture of Faith; one that I didn't ask for. Each year that we lost a child, Dan bought me a Christmas ornament of a girl angel that represented the baby we lost. After losing Faith, I decided to go in search of an ornament. I walked the aisles of a Hallmark store in search of an ornament but was having no luck. As I made it to the very end of my search around the store, I found it! It jumped out at me as headlights on a dark road! It was a beautiful, little, angel girl, holding a nest with birds and she had wavy, red hair. I knew that this was the ornament and felt that God had led me to it.

When I got home and opened up the box, I found a picture card of the girl portrayed in the ornament. I was so surprised to find that the girl on the card looked exactly as if it came out of the picture card that I had of my three girls. I know that it sounds as if I've made up this story, but I assure you it is true.

My story doesn't end there however, because there's Danny. Not long after my miscarriage with Faith, I shockingly became pregnant again. Weeks after the news, I was walking out of church when I stopped to view the free handouts on a table. My eyes fell on a small booklet which bore a picture on the cover of a small, curly, reddish-brown haired boy. He was on his knees praying, with a young angel girl standing over him. I was so attracted to this picture, like a nail to a magnet, that I took it home. I didn't know why I kept it, but thought that maybe it was God's way of letting me know that I had a boy growing in my womb.

Not long after, I miscarried again. I felt that his name was Danny. In my mind I call him Danny Boy. Again I received confirmation that Danny was his name, and thus now I had a boy in heaven. Everywhere I turned I was hearing the term Danny Boy. I remember walking into a department store and hearing the song entitled, "Danny Boy." On another day, I heard the name while at the vet where I had taken my cat. I happened to meet a woman who introduced her dog to me whose name was Danny Boy.

Soon after, I remembered the picture I found in church of the little boy. As I went to look at it, I noticed for the first time that the little boy had wings! I hadn't noticed it before! It was another confirmation that I had a boy. Another thing I noticed about the picture is that the boy looks a lot like the girls from the first picture.

I know that some believe in coincidences and others in God incidences. I happen to be a believer of the latter. All of these unusual events I feel are God's way of letting me know that He has everything in control; that He is with me and knows the desires of my heart. It makes me trust in Him and lean on Him when life gets difficult to bear. I have to believe that the better idea was for my four unborn children to abide like angels in heaven with their Maker, and I trust that I will meet them one day face to face.

As much as I tried to have a healthy, happy marriage, it failed. There were many obstacles in my relationship with Dan. Some had to do with the unhealthy habits I had derived from my childhood, such as the fear of intimacy. Others had to do with Dan's unhealthy habits or "baggage", and still others surfaced in the raising of our children. It was never easy no matter how hard I prayed.

To this day, I try to go over things in my mind to try to figure out why our marriage didn't work out. I feel that we might have had a stronger marriage if Dan and I prayed together more and sought God for strength and wisdom. We at times attended daily Mass together, but that usually didn't last. Even then, we did not pray out loud together, and I feel that it would have helped.

Intimacy was one of my issues that stemmed from the sexual abuse. At one time it became clear to me a pattern at bedtime. I believe I instigated it to keep my husband and me from being intimate. I very frequently started an argument right around the time we would be getting ready for bed. You've heard the well known phrase "Don't let the sun go down on your anger," (derived from Ephesians 4) but I lived as if the opposite were true. Because I was angry from our fight, it gave me an excuse to push myself to the very opposite side of the bed, facing away from Dan. This allowed for none of the warm but vulnerable moments that I felt uncomfortable with, nor did it allow for sexually intimate moments which only stressed me out.

Sexual relations were not fun for me for many reasons—the biggest being that I subconsciously associated the times with my husband with the times when I was abused. I know that this issue in my marriage was definitely a factor that hindered it because I've heard from friends and read from experts that sex is an essential element in a healthy marriage.

Another factor that affected my marriage was that the chemistry or dynamics between us changed. For the final two years of my marriage, and for the two years following my divorce, I attended a 12 step support group called CoDA, for people with codependency issues. I knew that I had habits that were exactly that. Habits or behaviors are very hard to change, especially when you've been doing them all of your life, and maybe were learned from your parents. I knew that I couldn't change my unhealthy habits with my own strength, so I attended this support group whose basis for change came from relying on one's higher power, mine being God.

In the meetings we read the 12 steps, which are listed in the book *Co-Dependents Anonymous,* and we discussed each step as we worked to lose our unhealthy behaviors. These behaviors were often survival mechanisms learned in our abusive or neglectful families as a child. We also learned about healthy boundaries and behaviors when relating to those around us, especially with those whom we are close.

I went to this support group faithfully every week and worked the program. I noticed healthy changes in my behaviors after my first meeting so I knew it was affective. I asked Dan to attend the meetings but he chose not to. He voiced his opinion that he didn't want me to go which I felt was due to his insecurities. The bad news is, as I was changing, Dan was staying the same—but not entirely.

As I interacted differently to him, it caused him to act differently towards me, but in a negative way. I shared this fact with the group and all that was transpiring in my relationship with Dan. The others responded that it was a common factor in members of

12 step programs. The dynamics of the relationship change. I went to CoDA weekly and professed to the group that no matter how difficult it got, I would never divorce Dan. I often spilled my heart out while tears streamed down my face. I wanted it to work and I prayed and begged God to make it work. Things seemed to get worse instead.

Another conflict in our marriage had to do with our son Christopher. From the age of three, I started to notice behaviors and moods that I felt were not "normal." I based my opinion on twenty years' experience dealing with children, as well as on my knowledge from an education degree. The most difficult symptom was the fits of rage, which came without warning, lasting an hour, and on some days, happened more than once.

In a fit of rage that might've been spurred on by dropping and breaking his Lego figure, Christopher would become violent. He would scream, cry, use bad words, throw things and aggressively lash out at those around him. He could destroy the entire house in a matter of five minutes. I often had to restrain him, and found it quite difficult, even at the young age of five.

For the next three years I read everything I could get my hands on including books from the library as well as articles online. I learned of different behavior management techniques and implemented them with Christopher, although nothing seemed to make his behaviors change. I began logging his behaviors on a daily basis, and after doing this for several years, I realized that his behaviors were cyclic. They worsened during the change of the seasons, as well as at any time when there was a significant change in his life, such as the end of the school year and beginning of summer vacation.

Other things that I did to try to help Christopher was to take him to a child counselor who helped him to deal with his emotions, specifically the anger that seemed to well up and flare into a fit of rage. Counseling helped but it still wasn't the cure-all. Even though Christopher and I were learning tools of what to do when we (I) saw a fit coming on, the emotions frequently flared too quickly for us to implement them. It's as if his anger went from zero to ten in a matter of seconds. I also felt that I needed emotional support as Dan was not available to me in this way.

I discovered a support group at Bradley Children's Hospital that was for parents of children with difficult behaviors. All of the parents there had a child diagnosed with some sort of mental disorder, many of which were bipolar. This group was a tremendous support to me emotionally. I benefited from "airing out" my frustrations and from hearing what the others had experienced and were still going through. I also learned from what they found useful in helping their children.

When Christopher was five years old I'll never forget the words he spoke to me. He was calm and we were having a loving moment as he sat cuddling in my lap. My baby said to me, "I hate myself." I began to address his feelings when he repeated those words a mother does not want to hear her child say. My heart was breaking for my boy and all I wanted to do was stop it from happening.

The symptoms that I noticed in Christopher seemed to fit that of a child with Early Onset Bipolar. By the time Christopher was six I felt sure that this is what he had. I honestly came to a point that I felt there was no reaching him without medication. I felt that there was a chemical reaction that was occurring in his brain that kept him from thinking in the moment and becoming aware of his emotions. It was as if when in a fit or episode my Christopher was gone and another person was in his place. Once he came out of a fit he was very apologetic and felt shameful for the things he had done. It was then that he realized, "Oh, I broke my favorite toy!" or "I kicked my own dog Baby!" or "I hurt my Mommy!"

I knew of a friend who had a child with bipolar and she referred me to her child's psychiatrist of whom she spoke very highly. I took Christopher, who was six at the time, to this doctor. He was evaluated by him, as well as the group psychologist. Both gave the same diagnosis—Early Onset Bipolar Disorder. The doctor prescribed a medication that, from the very first week, made a tremendous difference in Christopher's behavior and moods. As a matter of fact, the fits of rage ceased. I was so grateful to God for leading me to this doctor and medication for

Christopher. I prayed my heart out asking God to heal him. I truly believe that the healing came from the medicine created by man, who was created by God.

There were many changes in our home from that point on. From this time forward, I worked at building up Christopher's self-confidence. I believe he is a different child today at the age of twelve because those around him have been able to focus on his positive traits and the good things that he does. We also had more time to give to Gabriel who behaved like the "dream" child. Unfortunately, most of our time and energy was going to Christopher prior to the diagnosis. The biggest change though, came in the form of Dan and me getting divorced.

When I was in the support group at the children's hospital, I had shared the difficulties that my husband and I were having over the issue with Christopher. Members of this group in turn shared with me that it was very common for marriages to struggle through this type of problem and that many led to divorce. The underlying cause of division in the couple is denial of the child's illness and it is most common in the father of the child.

In our case, all I wanted to do was fix the problem and make it go away, and all Dan wanted to do was pretend the problem didn't exist. We tried resolving our conflict by seeing a counselor but we found it to be ineffective. This issue was the final issue, that when added to all of the rest, brought our marriage to an end.

I do not wish to go into details about how this came to be because I do not wish to say anything damning about Dan. I realize that "it takes two to tango." However, I felt that there was no other way to get our son the help he needed, as his father had become a block to this end. I felt that I had to advocate for our son, as he was only a child and unable to do it for himself. We, his parents, were entrusted by God to care for all of his needs, be it physical illness, which is more easily accepted, or mental illness.

For three years I tried everything I could to deal with the issue of our son and make our marriage work, but I found no other way but to meet with an attorney. I asked Dan if we could separate peaceably but he was unwilling. In meeting with an attorney I was hoping that Dan would see the seriousness of the situation, change his view and go along with getting Christopher professional help, but it didn't come to pass.

Once Dan and I divorced, my first thought was that I felt liberated because there would be no more fights with Dan. With Christopher being diagnosed and behaving in a peaceful, even joyful way, life in the home was a peaceful place to be. Dan and I were given 50/50 joint custody, with a court order forcing

Dan to give Christopher his medication. Even though it was difficult to not be with my children for half the week, I learned that it was a good decision. Because my boys got to see their Dad frequently, they didn't grieve the loss of their father, as many children experience.

Dan has purposefully maintained his residence within ten minutes of my home and therefore has retained a close relationship with his boys. This I am very grateful for and feel that it is one of the reasons why the boys did not suffer to the extent that they could have.

I have noticed that kids often go through a horrific time with divorce due to the fact that the mother gets primary placement and thus the father takes on the role of absent or distant parent due to the visitation being limited, such as every other weekend. This causes the children to grieve from the loss of the relationship they once had with their father.

The boys proved to do very well, considering the circumstances. In school, their teachers were surprised after they were told that Dan and I were no longer together. The boys never behaved in a way that made their teachers think that they were troubled. The boys continued to receive A's and B's in the following years. I believe that a part of them was relieved as I was, not to have to experience the continuous fighting that was happening between the two people they loved most.

Following the divorce, I tried as best I could to get myself and the boys the emotional support we needed. I entered a divorce support group that my church was holding and found it to be quite beneficial. I was pleased that my church didn't have a condemning attitude toward its members who divorced. Unfortunately, this is something that I have faced in many people including friends who were part of my (our) life for a decade. I met and became very good friends with another member of that group. I feel that she was a God-send; an angel that was there for me throughout that difficult period, and I her.

I got the boys support by taking them to a counselor. I took them every week for several months, until the counselor told me that she felt there was no longer a need. I made sure to talk with the boys about the divorce and read to them children's books written on the topic. I didn't want them to stuff their feelings inside, knowing it would only harm them in the long run.

Sometimes you hear of someone who loses a loved one through death and at the same time they are rejoicing because another loved one is carrying a new life. This seems like such a common phenomenon that it makes one wonder about the marvels of God, the author and finisher of life. As my boys and I, and Dan were grieving a loss as of a death, we were brought to rejoicing because we were expecting new life!

Dan and I tried for a third child for years without success and with no medical explanation for it. At a time when one would think it is the worse time, God thought differently and gave us Richard. I found out I was expecting in the middle of the divorce process, but it wasn't to be a cause for change—the divorce became final. However, in the midst of this hardship, the birth of our bundle of joy was a blessing.

If I were to describe Richard in one word, it would be "JOY." My favorite song to sing to Richard as a baby was "You Are My Sunshine" because he literally brought light and warmth to my wounded soul. I have no doubt that he did the same for his older brothers and father. For all of his five years he has woken with the dawn with a smile on his face and a song on his lips. Richard sings from sunrise to sunset. On those difficult days in the beginning when I was feeling blue, Richard's presence would bring me out of myself and his joyful way would lift my spirit. Richard has not only been a giver of life and love, but also a recipient. He has been "loved up" by our family to the extent that someone might describe him as being spoiled rotten.

Another support to me during the divorce process was my CoDA group. I continued to attend CoDA meetings weekly for another two years. I found emotional support and further guidance in such matters as "Why do I do the things I do?" "Why am I afraid of being intimate?" "What should I look for in a mate in order to have a healthy relationship?" I discovered so many things about myself.

One such example is the fact that I married a man that was like my father and brother. I had unhealthy relationships with them, and so it was likely that the same would be true in my relationship with Dan. I'm not saying that Dan was a lot like them, but he did possess traits that were familiar to me, and as the psychology books say—we marry a person like our parent because we are subconsciously trying to resolve issues of conflict that stemmed from our parent/child relationship. There were other co-dependent issues that caused dissension, ones that we each brought to the relationship. The difference between us was that I was willing to make changes and Dan was not.

All throughout the divorce process and the grieving that I went through, I felt that God was right there beside me. He continuously showed me His presence, which gave me strength, courage, consolation and peace. During that period, I spent much time in prayer, soaking in the love of God and claiming the promises of God. There were two particular verses that I felt God led me to cling to, one of which is from Zephaniah 3:14-17, "Sing O daughter of Zion; shout, O Israel! Rejoice, be in high spirits and glory with all your heart O daughter of Jerusalem...The King of Israel is in the midst of you...In that day it shall be said to Jerusalem, fear not, O Zion, let not your hands sink down or be slow and listless."

The other verse was an answer to prayer. God led me to the verse that states "Guard me as the apple of your eye" (Psalm 17:8). I had always desired to be the apple of someone's eye. A little girl desires this from her father, and when she doesn't get it, she seeks it from a mate. I had cried out to God, especially now that I was single again, and I actually told Him, "I want to be the apple of someone's eye!" God was telling me, "Holly, you are the apple of *My* eye." That thought put joy in my heart, as well as another verse found in Psalm 17:15 which says, "On waking, I shall be content in Your presence." This I also claimed and so I am happy to say that depression had no part in my life during this particular hardship.

I have another memorable story from this time in my life involving a day that I attended a Christian women's breakfast. It was on this day that our Lord spoke to me through a stranger when He said to me, "Let Me take the wheel as you sit in the passenger's seat and let me drive." I drew comfort from those words and received a confirmation that they were truly from God.

The same evening of the retreat I came to hear those very words as I channel-surfed the TV and came upon Carrie Underwood singing, "Jesus Take the Wheel." It was the very first time I had heard that beautiful song, and you can see why that song holds a very special place in my heart. This story shows just one of the many ways that God revealed Himself to me at this time, and from where I drew my strength.

    I knew that God had a plan for my life, one where He would restore me and my life. This assurance is what gave me peace of mind. When I told a friend that I was in the midst of a divorce, her face registered shock, and when I questioned her about it, she said, "You just seem to have such a peace about you. I never would've guessed it." It was true that I had peace, and also joy and hope. Looking with the natural eye, one would not see the reason for it. With the natural eye, a person would see a disastrous situation: a stay-at-home, single mother of two small boys and one on the way, with no job or savings to her name, and very little family support. But I had God and so I had everything. I put my trust in Him to provide for all of my needs and those of my boys.

Waves of Glory

"Did I not tell you that if you believe you will see the glory of God?" John 11:40

Chapter Twelve

It is the stroke of midnight. We embrace and kiss with a romance like that found in a Cinderella storybook. The floating fires dot the river about us...the live band is playing its celebratory music...my heart feels moved by the vibrations that are coming from the explosions of the fireworks which blast outside—but also inside. It is at this moment, on my second date with Steve, that I realize we will be together forever.

Back to the promise God gave me in Zephaniah 3. Verse twenty says, "At that time I will bring you home, and at that time I will gather you; for I will give you renown and praise, among all the peoples of the earth, when I bring about your restoration before your very eyes, says the Lord." It was three years later when I realized that God had kept His promise and restored my life. On the morning of my wedding to Steve, I knelt by my bed and sobbed my heart out in gratefulness to my God. I must have sobbed for a straight hour, thanking and praising God for His goodness and mercy toward me.

Steve and I met through the good ole World Wide Web. A year following my divorce, I started searching for a mate through online dating services. I knew several people including my cousin, who met their spouses that way. I liked the idea because my life didn't lend itself to meeting people in public venues. I was also very nervous about the idea of dating again as I hadn't done so in fifteen years. It was safe to view profiles of men and to meet them on the computer screen, and I could do it while being home and caring for my children.

I knew it might be difficult to find someone, considering the fact that I had three young children, but that didn't stop me from being hopeful. God restored my dream of having a healthy, loving, and peaceful family life, so I began praying for this and striving for it once again.

I was quite comfortable chatting with men online. It was much less strenuous than getting all dressed up and meeting in person. If I spent considerable time talking with a guy online ("phase 1" of my unique dating plan) and liked what I heard, then we exchanged cell phone numbers. At this phase ("phase 2"), I continued to get to know men while chatting on the phone and felt that I gained a lot more insight into the person in this way. Unfortunately, it weaned out just about all potential prospects, except for Steve.

Steve impressed me during "phase 1" and then continued to pull at my heart strings in "phase 2." He seemed real to me and not made up—as if to pretend he was someone he was not. I found him to be down-to-earth and a lover of the simple things in life, such as nature, which is also a love of mine. He was (is) thoughtful, sentimental, and had lived his life following God and His Word.

Steve made it to "phase 3" and so we met on our first date which was December 26, 2006. I was fortunate to have met my husband on my first official date since being single. I was saved from countless, unfulfilling, anxiety-filled dates with various men. Steve was not as fortunate as I, as he went through a dozen dates before meeting me and was ready to give up. Of course, that's when he met me.

Meeting people online also agreed with Steve's personality and lifestyle. He is a shy, conservative, family man who also found it difficult to meet or "pick up" women in public venues. We both desired to continue living the family life, and felt uncomfortable living the single life. We were so relieved when we didn't have to date any other person and looked forward to dating each other for the rest of our lives.

On the eve of our first date, I met Steve wearing a pair of gag glasses which made my eyes appear as if I were wearing coke-bottle glasses. At first sight, Steve was stopped in his tracks as he took a moment to decipher if I were "for real." My ploy at creating an ice breaker was a successful tactic. We greeted one another with laughter instead of a bundle of nerves.

As I was beginning life anew, I decided to live life to the full. Divorce was like a near-death experience for me and it completely changed my view on life. I realized that I had taken life too seriously until then, and hardly enjoyed the ride. My new motto in life which became "our motto" is LIVE (life to the full), LOVE (unconditionally), and LAUGH (until your belly hurts). The scripture verse that God showed me is "I have come that they might have life and have it to the full" (John 10:10). Through this verse, God made me realize that He wants me to be happy and to enjoy life.

Following our glorious second date on New Year's Eve, I can think of two other momentous occasions with Steve that assured me that he was right for me. The following Saturday, Steve called and asked me if I wanted to spend the day with him. I told him that I was going to spend it with my ailing grandmother at the nursing home. Steve shockingly told me that he wouldn't mind going along. I thought, *"How many people want to spend the day in a nursing home, especially when the person is a perfect stranger?"*

That day, as I watched Steve voluntarily push my grandmother in her wheelchair down the corridor, I had a sense that he and I would be together when we too were ailing grandparents.

The second occasion was when Steve, my boys and I were travelling and enjoying the sights of a quaint, country road. Gabriel excitedly pointed to the sky and shouted, "Look at that heart in the sky!" Sure enough, I looked up and saw the outline of the most perfect shape of a heart made out of clouds. It was as if God, the masterful artist Himself, painted this heart just for Steve and me as a sign that we were right for one another.

Our wedding day was set at Beavertail Lighthouse, one of RI's most picturesque locations. I was determined to have fun even on this day. Just before making my vows, I took out the gag glasses, the ones I sported that first date, and put them on. I only wore them for a quick second, just long enough to evoke some laughter, and indeed we all had a hearty laugh. We also made sure to include our motto within the words of our vows.

Steve and I have continued living life to the fullest. We have blended our families, which consist of my three boys and his youngest son. His two older daughters were already living on their own. We began our life by creating a cozy, country nest under groves of pine and oak trees. Our property reminds us of a sanctuary, or like the peaceful retreat places I've been to. Inside and outside our home, one is made to feel peace-filled and "at home." Many of our visitors tell us so.

Yes—God has led me to that place—"a land flowing with milk and honey" as He promised me all those years ago in the book of Leviticus. All my life I have desired to have a family life opposite of the one I had. I have prayed and worked hard to this end, and today I can honestly say it is so. God has "repaid the years the locusts have eaten" (Joel 2:25).

I rejoice and am blessed in my new life. I am grateful that I have been able to continue being a stay-at-home mother and so I am able to be there when my children come home from school. There has never been a moment when my kids were in need of their mommy and their need unmet. I tuck my boys in every night with a prayer, a kiss and a hug, even now when my oldest is thirteen.

My boys love Steve and have taken to him since the first day they met. There hasn't been a day that one of my boys has spoken a word of regret about my marrying Steve. As a matter of fact, they frequently take his side in matters of disagreement. My boys are happy and I believe it is because our home is filled with love, peace and joy, which inevitably come from God.

The boys and I recently traveled to Soul Fest, a Christian Music Festival in New Hampshire, and had such a good time. My oldest, Gabriel, 13, described his thoughts about it in a school essay. He wrote "My heart was thumping to the hammer of the base drum. My foot was tapping to the beat. My head was bobbing up and down to the electric guitars, and right at that moment, I felt like I was in the zone." The events of this day will remain in our memory banks for years to come.

Christopher,12, relives his memories of Soul Fest while listening to his Thousand Foot Crutch CD from the top bunk of his bed. It is when Christopher first heard of this band. He has been hooked ever since. Richard,5, is reminded of this day when he looks up at the framed photo on his bedroom wall taken the "day after" of a collection of our shoes completely covered in mud. This reminds him of the sucking, slurping sounds that followed each step we took in the foot deep mud we trod that day.

My memories are as follows...As the day approached to leave for the four hour drive, unfortunate things started to occur that made me doubt our going. My husband Steve couldn't go with us after all because he couldn't get away from work. That was a bit of an obstacle because I was relying on him to do the driving and help me with the kids. I didn't think that I could do it alone because of the fibromyalgia and chronic fatigue that I had. It kept me from doing most things that I wanted to do. In addition, Christopher was having a difficult time with things. On the eve of our planned departure, I hadn't even packed, and doubted that we were going to go.

The following morning we woke to a dark, rainy day. No matter what the negative circumstances were, there was something in me that was determined to pack up the kids and get to Soul Fest. I was driven by the desire for my musically inclined pre-teens to experience the God that I know and love, and the desire for them to know and love Him too. It rained so hard on the drive up that it was difficult to see the road at times. But we made the best of it while blasting the bands that we were going to see Live, such as Natalie Grant and Casting Crowns.

We finally made it to the four-day festival. We hesitatingly got out of the car and found that the rain clouds held no mercy for us—only buckets of rain water. Gabriel's first remark was, "Mom, can we just go to Grammy and Grampy's (an hour away)?" I couldn't believe he had the gall to ask that question—after spending one hundred dollars worth of tickets for one day, and all that I had to do to get us there. I told Gabriel just that. We left most of the luxuries that we brought in the car, such as chairs to sit on. I thought, *"What good would they do us if they were soaking wet? We'd just be sitting in puddles of rain water."*

Thank God my neighbor let me borrow an all-terrain stroller to push Richard in. He never would've gotten out of the car because of the mud if I hadn't. We observed some children his age sinking to their knees in mud. As I trudged Richard through the deep mud, I heard one mother say, "What are we doing here? Are we crazy?" For us parents who packed up our children and their entire gear—yes, we are crazy—crazy in love with Jesus Christ, and want the same for our children.

One of my fondest memories occurred within the first few minutes of our arrival, and that set the mood for the rest of the day. I wanted my kids to be happy in the midst of our circumstances, so I stopped and bought some Dippin' Dots for them to eat. Dippin' Dots are small, round, colorful pellets of ice cream. I thought, "*Ice cream does magic by bringing a smile to any child's forlorn face!*" Only the minute I gave Richard his cup of Dippin' Dots, he spilled it all over himself. The colorful, cold, melting pellets were now sitting in every crevice of his clothing and in the seat of his stroller.

I stood for a moment to catch my bearings. I almost freaked out, but then I looked at my older boys and remembered that this was supposed to be a fun experience. In the next moment, I followed my childish instincts. I picked the Dippin' Dots off of Richard, and chucked them at my older boys, kicking off a food fight. I then said, "When life tosses you lemons, you make lemonade." This was my motto to live by that day.

I wasn't the only one living out that motto. The boys and I came upon a few teen guys who were challenging each other as to who could run and slide the farthest in the wet, slimy mud. Their efforts left them covered from head to toe in mud, yet they were having a blast. Others took advantage of a gush of rain water that had caused a stream over a path of gravel. Instead of hopping over the little river, people would step into the water to rinse off the mud that was caked onto their shoes. Some people took off their shoes to rinse their feet. And some of those people just decided to walk around with bare feet, with the thought "*What's the use of wearing shoes?*"

The first band we saw was Thousand Foot Crutch. (Richard says, "Thousand Foot *Crunch*.") No chairs, no covering—just rain and mud. But, we made the best of it. Richard stood on the foot rest of his stroller practically dancing his head off, while Christopher became inspired by this particular band. Yes!!! This band is a much better choice than Ozzy Ozbourne, which is what he had gotten turned on to while playing Guitar Hero. Afterwards, we ventured to buy a Thousand Foot Crutch CD and T-shirt for Christopher. One-track minded Gabriel then says, "Can we go now?" I went on my spiel again and reminded them that we especially came to see Natalie Grant and Casting Crowns, and had yet to see them.

Thankfully, we found the only indoor stage where we could sit and find relief from the rain. This stage featured Christian rap music. As I looked around at the youthful crowd, I felt inspired to see so many young folk listening to lyrics that speak of Jesus as Lord, His Word, and all that He promises. Therefore, I enjoyed even this experience, as well as the stage that featured Heavy Metal. The good news is my children were the ones to want to leave that stage first. No argument there.

Miracle of miracles...The rain stopped! "*Thank you Lord*!" was the thought of thousands, especially those who had been camping out for days in the rain. I heard one of the campers whose tent was on the ski slope say that he had a river running through his tent each night. The rain stopped just in time for the main performances. At 6:30 p.m. the presenter came out to welcome Natalie Grant and spoke a few words about the weather. He said that a live, satellite, weather report stated that it would rain non-stop throughout the evening, and yet we had no rain above us. As Natalie sang out her songs, the sun came out from behind the clouds. We got to watch the sun set amidst a colorful, picturesque sky as we listened to Natalie sing about the *One* who created it.

The view remained spectacular as Casting Crowns came on stage and sang to us under a starry sky, lit by the bright light of the moon. I might've been the only one looking in the sky and capturing photos of it as the other viewers' eyes were on the stage. But I was keenly aware that God had blessed all those who stuck it out through the miserable weather conditions. The signs were in the sky.

That evening as I lay my exhausted, but contented body down, I offered a prayer of thanksgiving. I thanked God that He gave me the strength to enjoy the day with my boys, and He also allowed me relief from pain. We had fun together and made happy memories—ones that bind us together with chords of love.

Only two weeks had passed since my adventure with the boys when God healed me of fibromyalgia and chronic fatigue. But God not only brought me physical healing while on my trip to Florida, He also brought me inner healing. One evening I began to sob and I didn't know why. A friend, seeing my tears, came over and began to pray with me. Through prayer, we felt that God was bringing about healing my wounded heart associated with Dan and our divorce.

I felt God urging me to forgive all of the ways that he offended me and to no longer hold on to the hurts and bitterness that I felt he caused. God also urged me to forgive myself, which I never would've thought to do on my own. However, as I spoke the words, "I forgive myself," I sensed that I had a spirit of self-loathing for all of the ways that I hurt Dan during our marriage and then during the divorce process. I obeyed God on this evening, and afterwards felt such a peace in my heart. When I returned to RI, I noticed that I had a peace when I was around Dan which was not present before the trip.

This only confirmed what I have learned in the past—FORVIGNESS IS A GIFT. I make the choice to obey Him, and He does the work in bringing it about. Our Lord says, "My grace is sufficient for you—for my power is made perfect in weakness" (2 Corinthians 12:9).

From the time I was going through the divorce process to this day, I have been forced to reevaluate what I believe as a Christian and how I choose to be called. Many folks I meet in my Christian circles ask me "What church do you belong to?" And because of my experiences in the last few years dealing with various churches, I've decided that when I am asked that question, I will reply, "I am a believer." "*I am a lover of God, and a follower of my Savior Jesus Christ.*" I do not wish to be characterized or judged because of the church I attend. I'd rather focus on the heart of the matter…that of following the great commandment to "love God with my whole heart, soul and mind, and to love my fellow neighbor as myself" (Matthew 22:37-39).

Following my divorce, I found a lack of the love that God calls us to. My friends from St. Charles of at least a dozen years were of no support. Some of them felt that I was wrong to go through with a divorce. Throughout the entire two-year, tumultuous process, my friends were nowhere to be found. They judged me without asking me what it was like to walk in my shoes.

Further complications arose for me with the Catholic Church regarding its law that if a person divorces, he must receive an annulment before he remarries. Otherwise, he commits adultery and can no longer receive the sacraments. Following my divorce and knowing that I wanted to remarry one day, I went through the annulment process. I wanted to follow the laws of my church and be in good standing. I spent several months meeting with my parish priest as we filled out the two hundred page (or so) application. In the end, I was denied. These two matters were disheartening to me.

I continued to attend the Catholic Church even as I married Steve, but we were not allowed to marry in the church. Six months into our marriage I became very ill, experiencing symptoms which left me debilitated much of the time. During that time of illness, I spoke to an old friend named Jill who was a devout Catholic. She said to me, "You are probably sick because you never got an annulment and you are committing adultery." She also referred to me as a "Lost Sheep" (Luke 15), as if I had wandered away from the Shepherd. Jill's words caused me much grief.

The truth was that I didn't feel far away from God. I felt the opposite. And I didn't feel that He was displeased with me either. I spent days and sleepless nights pondering my standing with God. This particular conflict however, was only one of the many that led me to lean in close to God for a whole year. It is when I sought after Him, wanting to know the truth and wanting to know His desire for me.

After I moved away from the Providence area to move to the country with Steve, we began visiting various churches in our area. There weren't many choices as we lived in a rural town. We had been doing this when I became ill. Because of my illness, I wasn't able to attend church very much, but when I did feel up to it, I needed a church close to home.

I frequently drove by this cute, little white church with a steeple on top, with no affiliation listed on the sign in front. I decided to try this church as it was only a five minute drive from home. Upon my first visit, I discovered the church to be of the Baptist denomination. It didn't bother me that things were done a bit differently than the Catholic Church. I met people there who loved God just like I did and they were kind to me. I saw people who desired to live out the Bible and strove to attain the likeness of Jesus, just like people from the Catholic Church.

At this point in time, I had a few Catholic friends, and now I had Baptist friends also. I found that each group felt that I was not saved. The Catholics felt that I wasn't saved because I was going to a Baptist Church (and committing adultery), and the Baptists thought I wasn't saved because I had not been baptized as an adult. I heard many Baptists say derogatory things about the Catholics, and visa versa. This hurt me because I loved my time as a Catholic. It was then that I received my salvation. It was there that I received much inner healing.

I knew of many dear and loving people who were Catholics and I couldn't say that they weren't saved. The same goes for my Baptist friends. I had a new friend I met after our move and she was Catholic. She knew I was going to a Baptist church and at times when we got together, she would try to change my mind and wished me to attend her church.

My friend found it hard to accept my faith because of the church I attended. I responded to her, as well as some of my Baptist friends, "Why can't you accept me for where I am at? Can you honestly say that you believe that I don't know Jesus and that I am not saved? Look at my life, and see how I live and breathe Jesus and His Word." I would encourage my friends to love me and accept me and my faith, just as it is, and to not judge me based on the church that I attend.

During the time of my illness, there were many Sundays that I was not able to attend church, as I was bedridden. However, even though I was not in a church building, I feel that I was able to commune with God from my bed. God met me there. And during those times, with little distraction from the busy schedules of life, He would speak to me and clear up the confusion that I felt in my mind, as to what church is right, and where I might belong.

God filled me with the knowledge that I was OK. He accepted me. I was not in the wrong, as I feared. I very much did not want to displease Him. I was so happy to have the confusion that I felt gone. In my mind I had been thinking that maybe I was in the wrong, as my church friends were telling me. In my heart, I felt that I was in a right place—close to Jesus and His heart.

I am in no way negating the fact that church communities are important. But the emphasis needs to be on the people therein. It need not be in the "name" we give the community, nor the rules or doctrines that founders draw up in order to distinguish church communities. We are all part of one body, and Jesus is the head. Paul tells us in 1 Corinthians 12:27

"You are the body of Christ, each one of you a part of it. There should be no division in the body, but its parts should have equal concern for each other."

After a year's time of attending the Baptist Church, I regained my health. At this time I decided to search for another church. I soon found myself attending a non-denominational church. I learned of this church from two of my friends who were members, whose faith I admired and whose judgment I trusted. From the first service I attended, I felt as if I belonged. Over time, and after getting to know the pastor and the members of the church, I found the love of God present in them. The focus in this church was the people and the importance of living out God's Word.

After a year of attending this church, I found myself thirsty for more. This scripture spoke to me at the time, "Let anyone who is thirsty come to me and drink. Whoever believes in me, as Scripture has said, rivers of living water will flow from within them. By this he meant the Spirit" (John 7:37-39). What was missing in this wonderful community was the Holy Spirit. I was experiencing the fullness of the Holy Spirit in my private prayer time, but would get to church and only experience Him to a very small extent. What I was longing for was what I experienced in my days with Fr. Randall at St. Charles, and I thirsted after it. I witnessed the fire of the Holy Spirit then, and have seen glimpses of it throughout the years since.

At this time in my life, I wanted to experience the Third Person of the Trinity in all of His fullness. I shared this with my Lord and felt Him direct me to another church that I had heard about from friends of mine. This church is also non-denominational, but also Charismatic (Pentecostal). Since attending there, I have experienced the fire and the power of the Holy Spirit that I was seeking. I find that with the power of the Holy Spirit living in me, I am able to overcome the things of this world that keep me from living the life of Christ. By His power, I witness miracles (interiorly and exteriorly) in others, as well as in my own life, such as my physical healings.

It is apparent that I have had experience with attending churches of various denominations. The thing that they all have in common and, which I feel is most important, is the fundamental truth of the Bible regarding Salvation through Jesus Christ. All of these churches are Christian and all make up the body of Christ.

Whatever the differences are between the Christian churches, they should not be a vehicle of division. That would be like the arm of the body cutting off its pinky toe, thinking that it is not needed or it doesn't belong. "God has put the body together giving greater honor to the parts that lacked it so that there be no division in the body, but that its parts should have equal concern for each other" (1 Cor. 12:24,25). Therefore, no church should behave as superior to another in thinking that it has all the right answers, or that it is the one true church, and all others are inferior.

Because of the divisions and judgments going on with the churches, people are leaving the organized churches and meeting in their homes, just as in the New Testament times. I know of two such individuals, both friends of mine who now belong to home churches. Church for them is quite simple. A few folks come together in a home where they praise God in worship, study God's Word, and pray for the needs of one another.

When one such friend, Rose, serves in a local mission and is fundraising, she does not have to deal with the judgments of those who ask to which church she belongs, and face the refusal of a benefactor because her church is not his church, and thus not the true church. She shared her feelings on this matter with me and I had to completely agree with her. We've both decided to reply when asked that loaded question, "What church do you belong to (or religion)?" with the answer—"I am a believer." I believe that Jesus Christ saved me from my sins by dying on the cross. I believe that Jesus loves me and I will meet Him face to face in Heaven. I am a Christian, as the disciples called themselves following Pentecost.

Personally, I don't think God cares which of these churches I attend on Sunday. I think He cares more about the condition of my heart, and how I relate to my neighbor—saved or unsaved.

Chapter Thirteen

I hear those words of freedom once again, "Blackbird singing in the dead of night...take these broken wings and learn to fly." Minutes later, while in prayer, God set me free from twenty years of clinical depression and suicidal thoughts.

After Dan and I split up, I had this knowledge that I was going to write a book. I never heard an audible voice, but I felt that God told me, "You are going to write a book." I knew it to be true as I knew my name was Holly. My reply to God was, "OK. You just let me know *when*, and *where*, and *how*, and *what*." I believed Him, but with my natural mind, it did not make any sense. I didn't enjoy writing much and never took courses on the subject. I had absolutely no idea what I would even write about. However, two years later God revealed to me all of the details, and it occurred in the midst of my illness.

It happened on a quiet Saturday morning. I awoke and made my way downstairs to make breakfast for Steve and I. As I got halfway down the stairs, it occurred to me, "I'm going to write my book today." I hadn't even been thinking about it prior to this moment. Because I was ill, I had no plans that day, so upon finishing my breakfast, I sat down at the computer and began writing my book based on the healing process that God took me through fifteen years earlier.

I sat for eight hours that day, and another eight hours the following day. By the end of the weekend, my book was ninety percent finished. One of the reasons for the speediness of it is that I had taken poems that I had already written in my journal during the healing process. The only thing left to do was write about the present time in my life which describes the fruit of the healing process.

These final writings came to me within a two week span as I went about doing my daily tasks. Pictures with stories or words kept forming very strongly in my mind until finally I would sit down and get them on paper. From the beginning of the book until the end, the words just flowed. I didn't have to stop and think about what I was to say, nor did I have to go back to make major corrections. My book is entitled *The Tin Man-The Voice of an Incest Survivor*. It is a short work containing poems, inspirational verses and vignettes which take the reader through my journey from victim to survivor.

I decided to lighten the topic of my book with beautiful photos of nature that Steve had taken over the years, as well as my original art work which also depicts the beauty in nature. Both Gabriel and Christopher are artistic, so I commissioned them to draw a picture of the Tin Man. The results were astounding. Christopher's picture was finished with watercolor and sits on the cover of the book. Gabriel's picture sits on one of the inside pages.

Gabriel also contributed a poem which he brought home from school the day before the printing of the book. He won a poetry contest with his poem entitled, "A Second Chance," and it clearly suited the context of my book. It is quite profound for a twelve-year old class-clown. I think that God had something to do with it.

For the twenty years that I struggled with depression I was walking with God. I believe He had His reasons for allowing this struggle in my life. One of the ways He taught me to cope with it was by reading the Book of Psalms. Over and over through the years, He reminded me to stay close to the Book of Psalms. Every time I read the Psalms, I felt my spirit lift. There I would find hope, strength and consolation.

I speak of having depression in the past tense and that is because God gave me a supernatural healing on April 2, 2010, Good Friday. I'd been taken anti-depressants all those years—but never again! No more waking up on sunny days with a dark cloud hanging over my head. No more negative thoughts that only steal my joy. No more feeling overwhelmed as if life is too difficult for me to handle. No more despairing. The blood that was shed for me on Calvary has set me free!

The month beforehand, on March 4th, Turbitt Ministries offered a day-long retreat and brought a visitor named Frank Kelly who possesses many spiritual gifts. This man prayed over me and spoke words of prophecy. His first words were, "God is going to lift your depression." This wasn't even something that I was asking God for.

Within the following weeks, God kept giving me scriptures that spoke of joy. One such verse is from Psalm 16: 11, "You make known to me the path of life; You fill me with joy in Your presence, with eternal pleasures at Your right hand." On March 8th while in prayer, God told me that He was going to lift my depression away forever—never to return—and that He was going to replace it with His joy—joy that bubbles from within and overflows. I wrote this down in my journal, believing it to be true.

On Good Friday, I was invited by a friend to attend a church event where International House of Prayer (IHOP) from Kansas City would be visiting. Within thirty minutes of praise and worship, I felt the presence of the Holy Spirit fall upon me which left me "resting in the Spirit." During this time, I heard in my mind the song, "Blackbird." Ironically, three days prior, I woke with this song in my mind. I knew it meant freedom from something. I had asked the Lord what He meant by it, but didn't receive a reply. So again, the song came to my mind.

I knelt down, and soon began to weep, which lasted at least twenty minutes. I then became calm and returned to my chair. At this time, a student from IHOP gave a testimony about how he came from a life of abuse, including incest, all of which came at the hands of his parents. He spoke about living with depression, and at times, suicidal thoughts. He spoke about how one evening God delivered him from depression. During this time, he saw a sheet that had been over him, lift right off. For four years until the present, he had been free of depression.

Praise and worship continued, and soon I began to cry uncontrollably—harder than the first time. I didn't know why I was sobbing. Two students from IHOP asked to pray with me, and as they did, I continued to sob. They brought up depression and asked me if I had ever had suicidal thoughts. It was then that I knew what the Lord was doing in me.

While sobbing, a thought came to me about my mother and how she delved into witchcraft when I was a child. I spoke of this to the girls, and then they prayed. We renounced all curses; hexes; arrows; all holds or bondages that the devil had on my life. Finally, I saw a sheet being lifted off of me as we prayed, just like the man who gave his testimony. Altogether, we prayed, and I cried, for at least an hour.

As our time was concluding, I felt like there had been a battle and the victory had been won. I felt light as a feather, as if weight had been lifted off of my shoulders. I then saw myself as in a vision—just my face, with a radiant light, looking up, and filled with joy. My heart was filled with immeasurable joy!

This joy and peace has been with me ever since—two whole years now. I wake up regularly with a joyful song in my heart and can't wait to get on with my day. I owe it all to my Lord and Savior; my Healer and my Deliverer. My days aren't perfect and neither am I. I still get angry and sad at times. But these moments pass rather quickly, and I don't get to feeling overwhelmed. It was all in His timing. And I trust that He had a purpose. I am so grateful to Him for bestowing on me His mercy at this time.

Pat Turbitt always begins her talks with women with the words, "We are the beloved daughters of the Father." I have heard her say this numerous times over the last twenty years and only recently at the age of forty-four, did my heart come to believe it. At a recent Christian conference, God set me free from the lie that I had believed from the time I was born... "*I am of no value. I am unlovable and no good.*"

Weeks before the conference, God began to speak to me about my true identity, which is found in Christ. One day as I was shopping in a consignment store, my eyes fell on a book called, *Love Letters from Your King* by Sheri Rose Shepherd. I asked of its price and the owner of the store told me I could have it at no cost. I thought, *"Thank you Lord,"* as I felt that it was a gift from God. Within the weeks that followed, I read one entry a day, until it was time for me to travel to Florida for a National House of Hope Conference. I had no idea that I was to meet the author of that little book once there.

The entire time during the conference, God spoke to me and dealt with me regarding my identity. First, a friend had been telling me that she had spoken recently with a child friend all about the truth of her identity. "God is our King, and He has made us His children. So, as His daughter, you are beautiful, special, and of much value—just as a princess." She knew this because God tells us so in His Word, "The Spirit himself testifies with our spirit that we are God's children. Now if we are children, then we are heirs—heirs of God and co-heirs with Christ" (Romans 8:16, 17).

As my friend was relaying her story to me, I had no idea that God had prompted her to share it with me. I felt that I already had the knowledge of what she was saying. As we concluded our conversation and entered into another presentation, God would bring to my heart the truth that had only lived on the surface of my mind.

The speaker, Brian Molitor from Malachi Global Foundation, began his talk with, "I feel that God wants to bring freedom to some of us here today." He then went into detail on the topic of "Sonship." He pointed out what God's Word says on this topic, "God sent his

Son...that we might receive adoption to sonship. Because you are his sons (daughters), God sent the Spirit of his Son into our hearts, the Spirit who calls out, *'Abba*, Father.' So you are no longer a slave, but God's child; and since you are his child, God has made you also an heir" (Galatians 4:4-7).

Brian concluded his presentation with, "Let's allow some time for God to minister in our hearts today." As we sat and welcomed the Holy Spirit to move amongst us and bring freedom to the places in our hearts that were bound, I began to sob.

In a room of two hundred people, I sobbed uncontrollably as I felt the pain that accompanied my feelings—the ones that I felt as a baby, newly born. I became aware of the feelings that neither my mother nor my father behaved as if they cared that I existed. I felt the pain from not being loved and cared for by them, which left me feeling that my life had no value. Several people came over to pray with me and minister to me, and many words of healing and truth were spoken over me.

Eventually, I had an awesome vision of myself, again as a baby. But this time, God my Father received me as I entered the world. He put a royal robe around my shoulders and a crown on my head, and told me that I was His princess. He also told me that He loved me and thought I was special.

On the evening concluding the conference, the final speaker was introduced. We welcomed Sheri Rose Shepherd, author, speaker and former Mrs.

United States, and Miss Idaho. Sheri's testimony reveals how God spoke to her heart the truth about her identity which helped to transform her troubled life, and this became her inspiration to writing a series of books on this topic. It didn't occur to me until I got back from Florida that the Sheri who spoke at the conference, was the woman who wrote the book that I had been reading prior to my trip. If I had known ahead of time, I would've brought the book to get it autographed!

Following Sheri's talk at the conference, I got to meet her and her family. When I met her eight year old daughter, I noticed she had been wearing a princess crown-pendant around her neck. She was probably given that necklace as a reminder that she is a beloved daughter of the King. I admired this necklace, and secretly wanted one just like it. God knew my heart, and was to fulfill this desire of mine within a week's time.

Upon my return from Florida, I prepared to go away the following week with my husband to celebrate our anniversary. While on our seaside vacation, we did some window shopping. We entered one store that had ornamental jewelry made from ocean-type pendants such as sea coral or stones. With this in mind, I don't know what prompted me to ask if they had any royal-crown pendants. The sales clerk responded with, "No, I don't think we do." However, in the next moment I looked down and my eyes fell upon a crown-pendant necklace which lay under the clear glass of the counter.

I asked to look at this beautiful sterling silver necklace. The crown was filled with cubic zirconia, which sparkled like diamonds. Steve saw how much I liked this necklace and said to me, "Well, I was going to buy you a watch for your anniversary gift (my last one had just broken), but if you'd prefer this necklace then I will buy it for you."

I chose the necklace over the watch and have worn it every day since that day in the store. Since then, I almost never know what time it is, but I always know who I am in Christ. As I walked away that day wearing my new necklace, I knew that God my Father, who had set me free from the lie that the devil had fed me, had given me a gift. I walked away from that jewelry store wearing my crown, with my hand in Steve's hand and my head held high, filled with the knowledge that I am a princess and heir to the King.

God has revealed His glory in my life most recently regarding my son Christopher. Christopher is the child who has been diagnosed with Early Onset Bipolar and has been receiving treatment, including the prescription of a very potent anti-psychotic drug called Risperdal. I am grateful for this medication because it has helped Christopher tremendously these past six years. Many times while Christopher was on the medication, I stopped to thank God that he experienced no apparent, negative side-effects. In concern for his future, I prayed an ongoing prayer— "Let Christopher have no lasting ill effects from the medication."

In the beginning, when it was evident that Christopher had special needs, I prayed to God for healing. As I sought God, I felt that He led me to a doctor, a diagnosis, and then the medication. All was a blessing! However, over the years I have continued to pray for Christopher's healing. I especially prayed in earnest while I suffered from my physical illness.

I found it very difficult to ask God to heal me, when my son also needed healing. This is when I began to pray for Christopher's healing anew. I prayed for him during my daily prayer time, as well as when I tucked him into bed at night. Sometimes I laid my hands on his head and prayed, to which he expressed no objection. I often sat beside his bed while he was sleeping. I would anoint his head with oil and pray that God heal his brain and the abnormal chemistry within.

Once God healed me, it became a testimony to Christopher of what God can do. I heard Christopher tell someone that I was praying to God and believing that God would heal him too. Once I heard him say, "Mom is *sitting* on her faith that I'm going to be healed." I knew he meant *standing* and this caused me to chuckle. Hearing him speak those words filled me with joy.

It seemed that once I was healed, I became even more determined to pray for the healing of my son. As I grew in physical strength, it seemed that I became stronger spiritually. I began praying more earnestly for Christopher. I feel that this was all God's doing. It was time—God's timing. God had brought us to a place of grace and mercy and compassion. He used me to bring about my son's healing.

God gave me a promise in regards to Christopher's healing. In Matthew 15:22, 28, a mother cried out to Jesus, "Son of David, have mercy on me! My daughter is demon-possessed and suffering terribly…then Jesus said to her, 'Woman, you have great faith. Your request is granted.'" I began to pray as this mother prayed and believing as this mother believed. As I prayed long and hard for Christopher, God brought me to a place of battling with the enemy. It was as if the enemy had a hold on my son. Because I am Christopher's mother and have authority over him, I was able to take authority over the enemy and command him to leave my son in the name of Jesus Christ (Luke 10:19).

Christopher's twelfth birthday had come. On that day, August 13th, while in prayer, I asked God my Father to have compassion on my son—His son. I asked of Him, "Would you please heal Christopher for his birthday gift? Would you please give him a new brain like that of a brand new baby—one that is healthy and new?"

Within a week's time, I went to Florida for another Christian conference. One day, while there, I began to pray for Christopher's healing, but then I heard God say to me, "It's been done." From that moment on, I stopped praying for Christopher's healing and began thanking and praising God for healing him. Once home from my trip, I asked God to let me know when I should start weaning him off his medication. Within a week or so I felt prompted to start, and thankfully, there were no negative side effects.

Another week past and then it hit me.

I received an email from a friend who had shared that he was extremely happy to announce that his brand-new baby granddaughter was to arrive any minute. His words were exuding with joy and quite contagious! His very last sentence said, "It is a day of miracles!"

At those words I began to sob…and sob…and sob. As I cried, I heard (felt) God say to me, "You asked Me to give him a new brain like that of a brand-new baby. And I have answered your prayer—*a mother's prayer*. You have prayed daily since the birth of each of your children that I make them 'Holy-Healthy-Happy.' Your prayer has been answered." I was hit with the realization that God brought His promise to fruition. I then became aware that my tears were of relief and utter gratefulness. Yes, it *was* a day of miracles!

Christopher has been off his medication and free of the hellish symptoms of bipolar illness for twenty-one months now. Alleluia! Words cannot describe my gratitude to God for setting my son free. My hope is to show my appreciation in the way that I love Him. I want to love Him to the best of my ability and please Him all the days of my life.

Where Are They Now?

Chapter Fourteen

Before I begin the Q & A session, I add one more topic which I feel is important to mention to my audience, and that is—Choices. "My choices have led me to a life of wholeness and freedom. They have led me to be a giver of life—in that I am able to nurture a healthy, loving family, as well as healthy friendships.

Most importantly, my choices have brought me to a place where I can call myself a survivor—a victim no more!" Can my siblings say the same thing? It is my prayer that God's mercy and grace may make it so. But...even in this, they must choose to receive His grace and mercy, as our loving Father has given us free will.

Today Bonnie and I enjoy sharing our friendship with one another's families. I am Auntie Holly to her three children, and she is Auntie Bonnie to my three children. We make sure to get together on Birthdays and special occasions, just like family. We are there for one another in times of need, or just to catch up with a cup of coffee. We are like family, and this is so appreciated because neither one of us has had the support of family. Bonnie was estranged from her family when she chose to not follow the life of a Jehovah's Witness. I suppose we both might be a gift from God. I like to think that I have blessed her life, as she has blessed mine.

Auntie has continued to be there for me just as a mother would, even though I am a married woman and have children of my own. I remember the day I saw Auntie following a miscarriage that I had. The moment we met each other, Auntie embraced me, held me tight, and wept with compassion for me. With each passing second that she held me, she brought healing to my broken, grieving heart. She has wept with me many more times since then, through the trials and celebrations of my adult years.

Auntie has continued to be there for me throughout the years, in the good times and in the bad. Just this past month she spent a few days with us in our home, and what a delight it was! She even graced us with her homemade cookies!

As I ponder the life of my siblings Michael, 47, and Elizabeth, 42, I am brought to think about choices. Each of our choices has led us to the place that we are today. I am sad when I think about the lives that my siblings have been leading their entire adult lives. I feel that the choices that they make for themselves only cause them further grief and misery.

I realize that our dispositions are different, thus affecting our behaviors and choices, but I feel that if my siblings had only turned to God for strength, comfort, and healing, much pain and sorrow could've (could be) been avoided. It's unfortunate however, that a child who grows up without the love and nurture from his parents, doesn't have the self-worth which would motivate him to make choices that are good for him, and which will cause him happiness.

My sister Elizabeth dropped out of high school in the ninth grade. She had learning disabilities that made it very hard for her to succeed academically, and she didn't have the support of my mother or my father to assist her. Not believing in herself, Elizabeth just gave up.

Around this time, she was hanging around with our two step sisters who were also very troubled (Their birth mother was murdered by her drug-addicted boyfriend). All of them spent most of their time partying, especially with guys. They were rarely home and when they were, there was no one to give them guidance or correction. My parents' focus was on each other and living a life of bliss, without the distraction of kids.

Eventually, Linda, 13, was kicked out, and Julie and Elizabeth, both 15, left home. Simultaneously, they all quit school. They never did return home, but spent the next few years living with various families of friends or boyfriends who would have them. Linda ended up in a home for wayward kids, as she got in trouble with the law various times.

When my sister was about the age of eighteen, she met a man who beat her. She became pregnant with his child and they eventually married. Elizabeth had two more children with this man. She remained with her first husband for many years, which was off and on, because they fought constantly.

Eventually, Elizabeth hooked up with another man who also beat her. S55he seemed to carry on Gram's legacy of having many husbands and being unfaithful to them all. By the age of forty, Elizabeth had married and divorced four times. Each of Elizabeth's husbands beat her. Her second husband held a gun to her head in front of her children during one of their daily disputes. Two of her husbands were former convicts, one of which she met while he was on work release.

Elizabeth became eligible for SSI (Supplemental Security Income) because she was unable to keep a job which was due to the presence of manic depression (now considered bipolar disorder by the medical field). Her depression caused her to have severe bouts with suicidal inclinations over the years. Elizabeth was given medication to remedy this, but unfortunately, she never liked the way the medicine made her feel, so she got into the habit of selling it to make money. Elizabeth also has an eating disorder called bulimia, due to the fact that she obsesses with her looks. She is always thinking that she is fat, when in fact, she has never been fat in her life. And lastly, she is an alcoholic.

Each of Elizabeth's children, one by one, left her to live with their grandmother, my mother. As each of her children approached their teens, they began to rebuke Elizabeth for her ways. They realized that she neglected them, always putting men and the bottle before them, and they came to disrespect and loathe her. Elizabeth has estranged herself from my parents and siblings. She hates my mother and won't have anything to do with her because she claims that my mother stole her children from her and turned them against her. Of course, this is far from the truth. Most apparent to me is that Elizabeth is holding a grudge with my mother and father for all of the things she wished they had done or not done.

My mother who had been neglectful to her own children seemed to make up for that by taking in and caring for her grandchildren. My mother and step-father also took in Julie's daughter Vicky. They became her legal guardians when she was around eight years old. The state had come to take her from Julie who was an unfit, drug-addicted mother. All of my nieces and nephew have been raised by my mother and step-father, and are now in their twenties and living on their own. Unfortunately, they too are making decisions that are not healthy for them. They, like their parents, grew up without the love and nurture of their mother and father. It's a vicious cycle.

On the other hand, because my brother Michael feared wounding his own children as he was wounded, he chose to never marry and have children. He made this decision in his twenties, and to this day at the age of forty seven, he is still single.

During high school Michael did very well. He got involved in a local church and came to love the youth group. Michael became a leader and mentor with the younger kids. He also was an excellent student. While I was out on the streets partying, Michael was in the house studying. It seems that his books became the place where he would escape his troublesome life. He graduated with high honors and received a full scholarship to a local university.

When Michael went to college, many things changed. Michael studied psychology as an effort to try to figure out and resolve life's hurts and troubles. He got involved with groups and studied extensively the topic of "violence against women." It was then that Michael decided there couldn't be a God, because what God would allow all of the suffering that goes on. And if there is a God, then he wouldn't want anything to do with Him. He also said to me, "If there is a God, then she is a woman." This comment came from the fact that he became very involved in equal rights for women.

He joined groups such as NOW (National Organization for Women) and others, which in part, call for the ERA (Equal Rights Amendment). My brother has become an advocate for women, which is a good thing, but not an advocate for unborn women, as he also involves himself with the Pro-Choice movement. His intentions throughout his adult years have always been good, but he nevertheless, has led a life which has promoted aloneness. This I believe is one of the causes of the depression and suicidal thoughts that he gets every so often.

Michael moved to the West Coast following college and has barely kept up communication with his family. We recently saw him when he visited the East Coast for the first time in ten years. He doesn't write or call anyone except my mother, which is about one phone call every few months.

Over the years, I've learned of his involvements and activities which lead me to conclude that my brother is very confused about his identity. He considers himself bisexual and has been known to cross-dress. He has been involved in New Age, witchcraft (the "good" kind), Native American beliefs, gay/lesbian rights, astrology, and currently administers healing to others through Reiki, which is based on an ancient Buddhist technique. Unfortunately, I believe that Michael has searched high and low to find purpose, meaning and happiness in his life, but has left out God, who is "the Way, the Truth, and the Life" (John 14:6).

In the worldly sense, Michael has struggled to support himself. He has continuously over the years been without a job, often trying to make ends meet with part-time employment. Every now and then he makes a call to one of our parents or me asking for money. Michael seems to throw himself into the causes in his life, spending forty hours a week as a volunteer, neglecting the fact that he needs an income to survive in this world. He moves from home to home because of his financial state. Even in his forties he has found himself without a place to live, being forced to depend on friends for lodging.

To this day, my siblings have yet to acknowledge molestation from my father, but Elizabeth can't even recollect when it happened with my brother, who has admitted it to me. She did share with me later as adults, that she had been molested several times by different people as a child. One such person was our neighbor and family friend. I found it easy to believe my sister because this father of three had always been touchy with me, and once "pantsed" me by jokingly pulling down my bathing suit bottom while swimming in the family pool.

I have no doubt that my siblings were both molested by my father. At least twice Michael told me that he had been going through some therapy and the issue had come up, but he still wasn't certain. Interestingly, I've learned from Michael that some of the seminars and conferences that he attends on behalf of feminist and gay/lesbian groups, offer workshops for the sexually abused. This is because the number of victims in these groups, to which he is a member, is so high.

When Michael does communicate with any of the family, he continues to bring up the past, reiterating all of the ways in which my mother and father damaged us children. Every time I communicate with my siblings, they both tend to air out their disappointments from childhood. This in turn saddens me and causes me to not want to relate with them at all. I have also found it difficult to relate with them because they frequently make choices that bring me offense, or to those whom I love. On the whole, I feel that they are unable to relate with others in a healthy way and this keeps them from having deep, personal, and loving relationships.

Both of my siblings find it hard to have a relationship with our father because he remains distant from them. My father self-righteously takes this position as if they deserve his neglect because of their bad choices and troublesome lives. My siblings desire our father's love and acceptance, but at the same time they still hold bitterness and resentment towards him because of his past offenses.

It is clear to me that Michael and Elizabeth have *chosen* to live as a victim, and this has kept them stuck in that wounded place, not allowing themselves to heal and move forward. They have held onto resentments, choosing to not forgive, and this has caused them to be bitter and depressed.

Elizabeth, Michael and I didn't have a choice when we were victimized as children, but as we matured and became adults, we did have the choice to either remain a victim or to live as a survivor.

  I try to give my father and mother a call at least every other week, if they don't beat me to it. They are both very good in keeping in touch with me and with sending cards and treats to the boys on special days of the year. Both of my parents live in Florida and are still married to my step-parents. Mom lives on the East Coast and Dad lives on the West Coast, so we don't see them very often. Mom came to stay a week with us this past fall, and we got to spend my father's birthday together in March. On that day I surprised my father with a small celebration at a local restaurant. My father was so touched by my attention to him and all that I had done, that he had tears in his eyes. It was a special moment for me.

  I don't want to paint a perfect picture of my relationship with my parents. Both sets of parents are very dysfunctional, to the point that I am glad that my children do not see them very much. My mother is known for coming to stay with us in our home, and my father does his traveling in an RV, so we don't have to feel pressured to have him stay with us. I love my father, but truthfully, I do not trust him to be with my boys alone.

Dad has never admitted his wrongs done to me, but there was an occasion that might have spurred my father's remorse. A few years ago my father and I had come together to mourn the loss of his father. Following the funeral service, as we all processed out of the church, my father came to me sobbing. He embraced me while sobbing like a baby. He sobbed so hard that his body was giving way onto my body so that I was having a hard time holding us both up. That is when my step-mother and father's siblings came over to pry my father off of me and lead him into the waiting limousine.

Since that occasion, I have pondered the actions of my father on that day, and have to honestly say that I don't know the reason. I do have a hunch however. I believe that my father was abused by his father, and upon the death of my grandfather, feelings arose to the surface regarding his own abuse. This in turn led my father to feel remorse for abusing me. I suppose I'll know for sure when I meet God face to face.

Afterword

"The hand of the Lord came upon me." Ezekiel 37:1

hand in Hand is meant to provoke the image of one placing their hand in another person's hand. The title which begins with a lower case "h" is meant to symbolize my hand, and the third word of the title which begins with a capital "H" is to symbolize God's hand. The feelings that the image provokes is one of trust. Certain pictures may come to mind as you think on this phrase, such as two lovers strolling on the beach, or two young girls—best friends, accompanying each other on the way to school, or a protective mother who takes her little boy's hand as they cross a busy street.

Within each of these images, there is a common element. Before a person takes his or her own hand and places it in the hand of another, trust is needed. It might sound ironic that I, who had once been abused, terrified and repulsed by hands would choose the title of my book using this image. The title of my book proves that God has healed my heart, and has filled me with so much of His love, that I have been able to trust in Him completely with my life. Trust was stolen from me by the evil one, but God restored it to my life.

Within the weeks that I pondered using this title, God gave me several stories and real-life images that had this similar theme. For example, one day while watching a detective show on the television; there was a scene of a small boy who had witnessed a horrific and terrifying crime. It caused him to run away where he came upon a dark, corner to hide in and feel safe. Eventually a detective found the boy and tried to speak to him with enough gentleness so that the boy would trust him and feel safe to leave with him. The man held out his hand to the boy hoping the boy would put his hand in his. The boy hesitated for a while, but eventually he did place his hand trustingly in the hand of the gentle man.

When I was born, God entrusted me to my parents. My parents, however, failed to be reliable and safe because of their own emotional deficiencies. God was aware of this and sent my Auntie into my life where He would use her as His instrument to love me and help me to feel safe. This brings to mind a conversation that I had in my twenties.

I was at a gathering with Christian friends and talking with a friend named Steve, who was very gifted by the Holy Spirit. Steve said to me, "I am having a vision of you as a little girl and beside you is an older woman who is holding your hand. God sent this woman to be a blessing in your life." I knew that the woman was my Auntie, and yes, I had always believed that she was like an angel sent by God. I hadn't remembered this conversation until recently, when I pondered using the title *hand in Hand*. Later in my teen years, God used my Nana as his instrument of love.

In those early years of my upbringing, God had reached out His hand through these two Godly women to care for me, love me, and help me to feel safe, until one day, I reached back. Since that time, I have found God to be reliable and trustworthy. I have found Him to be a loving Father who is always there for me, who never hurts me, and who wants only good things for me. I joyfully walk with Him, hand in Hand.

"They overcame him (the devil) by the blood of the Lamb and by the word of their testimony."
Revelation 12:11 NASB

www.ingramcontent.com/pod-product-compliance
Lightning Source LLC
Chambersburg PA
CBHW070639160426
43194CB00009B/1509